Lachlan T. CAMERON - Richard G. HENNING - Peter I. VACCARI

Pope Benedict XVI's
APOSTOLIC JOURNEY
to the United States
and visit to the United Nations

April 15-20
2008

Christ Our Hope

ÉDITIONS DU SIGNE – IGNATIUS PRESS

Catholic New York – Catholic Standard, Washington DC

With special thanks to Patrick Danczewski, Susan George, Mark Ruggiere, Matthew Schiller and John Woods for their generous cooperation in the making of this book

Éditions du Signe
1, rue Alfred Kastler - Eckbolsheim
B.P. 94 – 67038 Strasbourg, Cedex 2, France
Tel: 011 333 8878 9191
Fax: 011 333 8878 9199
www.editionsdusigne.fr
email: info@editionsdusigne.fr

Ignatius Press
2515 McAllister St.
San Francisco, Ca. 94118
phone 415-387-2324
www.ignatius.com

Publishing Director
Christian Riehl

Director of Publication
Joëlle Bernhard

Authors
Rev. Lachlan T. Cameron, MA, MDiv, ordained a priest of the Diocese of Rockville Centre in June 2008, currently serves in parish ministry.

Rev. Richard G. Henning, STD, a priest of the Diocese of Rockville Centre, is a professor of Sacred Scripture at the Seminary of the Immaculate Conception in Huntington, NY.

Rev. Peter I. Vaccari, STL, a priest of the Diocese of Brooklyn serves on the faculty of the Seminary of the Immaculate Conception in Huntington, NY.

Layout
Éditions du Signe - 107958

Cover picture
© CNS photo/Nancy Wiechec

Texts of Papal addresses, homilies, and official statements
© Libreria Editrice Vaticana

Table of contents

- Foreword by His Eminence Edward Cardinal Egan, Archbishop of New York

- Preface by His Excellency Donald Wuerl, Archbishop of Washington

Foreword

April, 2008

My Dear Friends,

The Apostolic Journey of Pope Benedict XVI to the United States was a moment of great grace for the Catholic Church and for all Americans. Over the course of six days, the Holy Father visited the Archdiocese of Washington, the Archdiocese of New York, and the United Nations. Before government leaders, clergy, religious, the Catholic faithful, and all people of good will, the Bishop of Rome witnessed to his own faith, and that of the Church, in Christ Jesus.

In his prayers, addresses, and personal interactions, the Holy Father's warmth and compassion touched countless minds and hearts. This was especially evident at Ground Zero, where he offered a moving prayer and comforted those who lost loved ones on September 11, 2001, survivors of the horrific attack, and those who heroically responded to save the lives of others.

This commemorative book chronicles the Holy Father's historic journey in words and pictures. These moving images bring to life the spirit of each of the remarkable encounters between the Holy Father and the people of the United States. Likewise, the text highlights the essential message of the Pope, a proclamation of "Christ Our Hope." In his homily at Yankee Stadium on the last day of his visit, Pope Benedict encouraged us to turn to Christ as, "the way that leads to eternal happiness, the truth who satisfies the deepest longings of every heart." It is my prayer that this book will assist each of us to meet this Jesus who is indeed "Christ Our Hope."

Very truly yours,

+ Edward Card. Egan

Edward Cardinal Egan
Archbishop of New York

Preface

April, 2008

Dear Friends,

The visit of our Holy Father, Pope Benedict XVI, was a time of grace for the Archdiocese of Washington, the Archdiocese of New York and the entire Church in the United States. The Pope's visit provided all of us an opportunity to renew our appreciation of our faith, the role of Peter in Christ's plan for his Church and the continuation of that ministry in the person of Pope Benedict XVI. As he said in his homily during Mass at Nationals Park, "As the Successor of Peter, I have come to America to confirm you, my brothers and sisters, in the faith of the Apostles."

From the time of his arrival on through every moment of the demanding schedule that our Holy Father kept, his warm and enveloping smile, his gracious kindness and his affirming and challenging teaching inspired all of us, bishops, priests, deacons, women and men in consecrated life and faithful laity. In so much of what the Pope said, he reminded us of the outpouring of the Spirit that is the source of the new Pentecost of which we are all a part and the importance of our participation in the life of the Church — the Body of Christ.

So many, including those who are not members of the Church, recognized how his presence and message so positively affected them. As he carried out his apostolic ministry, the Pope offered us direction and guidance so that we would be able to address the challenges of our contemporary society. He also reminded us that in light of all these challenges, we are to be evangelizers and people who bear witness to the gift of faith. His visit, message and confirmation of our efforts as a Church to be true witnesses to Christ are for all of us a source of affirmation and encouragement. This book should be a treasured keepsake of the Apostolic Journey of Pope Benedict XVI to the United States. May its pages be a constant reminder of the blessings we received from our Holy Father who came to bring us the message of Christ Our Hope.

Faithfully in Christ,

(Most Reverend) Donald W. Wuerl
Archbishop of Washington

April | 15-16

– Arrival at Andrews Air Force Base –
Prince George's County, Maryland
Tuesday, April 15th
4:00 p.m.

After months of preparation and planning, Pope Benedict XVI's chartered Alitalia Boeing *777*, designated *Shepherd One*, landed on a beautiful spring day at Andrews Air Force Base in suburban Washington, DC. The plane came to a halt before an excited crowd of more than 1,000 invited onlookers and an honor guard composed of representatives from the various branches of the United States Armed Forces.

Amidst mounting anticipation, the doors of *Shepherd One* opened and a red carpet was rolled out to the steps. Archbishop Pietro Sambi, Apostolic Nuncio to the United States, entered the plane and welcomed the Pontiff on his first Apostolic Journey to the United States. The President of the United States, George Bush, the First Lady, Laura Bush, and their daughter, Jenna, walked to the plane. When Pope Benedict appeared in the hatchway of *Shepherd One*, he had to clutch his white

■■■ Youth from nearby Bishop McNamara High School in Forestville, Md., cheer as Pope Benedict XVI arrives at Andrews Air Force Base.
© RAFAEL CRISOSTOMO, CATHOLIC STANDARD, WASHINGTON, DC

The Archdiocese for the Military Services, USA

Andrews Air Force Base, located in Maryland, is under the ecclesiastical jurisdiction of the Archdiocese for the Military Services. Created by Pope John Paul II in 1985, this non-territorial archdiocese provides pastoral services for more than 1.4 million Catholics serving in the United States Armed Forces around the world.

Archbishop Timothy Broglio was installed as the fourth Archbishop for the Military Services on January 25, 2008. Prior to this appointment, His Excellency served the Church for over 25 years, in various diplomatic missions, including eleven years in Rome (1990-2001) where he served as Chief of Cabinet for Cardinal Angelo Sodano, the Secretary of State. Having come to know the then Cardinal Ratzinger, Archbishop Broglio shared some reflections on the qualities of Pope Benedict in a press release on March 13, 2008:

*There is no question that the Holy Father perceives clearly his role
as teacher and evangelizer… His devotion to diligent personal study,
his responsibilities, and a very simple lifestyle characterized his manner
during the years that I witnessed his direction of the Congregation of the
Doctrine of the Faith… He is a kind man who looks intently at his
interlocutor and gives him his undivided attention…He has a clear
message and asks difficult questions…*

zucchetto as the wind threatened to blow it down the tarmac. Smiling broadly, he descended the stairs to greet President Bush and the First Family.

After a brief but warm exchange, other members of the Holy Father's retinue joined him and were received by the president. The Pope then greeted Cardinal Francis George, OMI, Archbishop of Chicago and President of the United States Conference of Catholic Bishops (USCCB), Archbishop Donald Wuerl of Washington, DC, and Archbishop Timothy Broglio of the Archdiocese for the Military Services. They and a number of other prelates offered the traditional *bacciamano*, the kissing of the apostolic ring.

As the Holy Father drew closer to the viewing stands, the crowd called out to him and he smiled and waved with both hands, clearly pleased by the warm welcome. Catholic school children sang "Happy Birthday," further delighting Pope Benedict on the eve of his 81st birthday.

President Bush joined the Holy Father in a nearby facility for a ten minute meeting with the assembled dignitaries. During the meeting, a presidential limousine arrived with papal and American flags displayed on its front bumper. The Holy Father reemerged with President Bush and the First Lady, walked to the car, and exchanged greetings once more before his departure for the Apostolic Nunciature, the embassy of the Holy See to the United States, in Washington, DC. Pope Benedict left Andrews Air Force Base in a motorcade accorded the same level of security as for a sitting president of the United States.

While the arrival ceremony was brief, it was truly historic, marking the first time that a president traveled to Andrews Air Force Base to greet a visiting leader. When questioned before the visit about this unusual welcome, President Bush asserted the uniqueness of this particular leader who comes to the United States as a man of faith, who represents millions, and who warns contemporary society of the dangers of moral relativism.

■■■ Arriving for his first pastoral visit to the United States, Pope Benedict XVI walks
with President George W. Bush past a military honor guard at Andrews Air Force Base.
© RAFAEL CRISOSTOMO, CATHOLIC STANDARD, WASHINGTON, DC

During his flight to the United States, Pope Benedict responded to questions submitted by the press corps. His Holiness spoke
about the scandal of pedophile priests, expressing his shame at
such sins and his determination to prevent future abuses. He also
signaled his intention to confer with the president about immigration and the concomitant tragedy of separated families. He went
on to praise the American innovation of the separation of church
and state, observing that this separation has served to protect the
free exercise of faith and provide space for religious and moral
viewpoints in political life.

With his arrival at Andrews Air Force Base and the historic
greeting by the First Family, Pope Benedict XVI embarked upon
his pilgrimage to America, a land of *"a great people and a great
Church."*

■■■ Leonarda Malyemezian, who is stationed at Bolling Air
Force Base in Washington, DC holds a small American
flag and her rosary as she awaits Pope Benedict's arrival
at Andrews Air Force Base on April 15.
© RAFAEL CRISOSTOMO, CATHOLIC STANDARD NEWSPAPER, WASHINGTON, D

■■■ The papal motorcade arrives at the Apostolic Nunciature
(Vatican Embassy) in Washington, DC on April 15 for
Pope Benedict XVI's first pastoral visit to the United States.
© MICHAEL HOYT, CATHOLIC STANDARD NEWSPAPER, WASHINGTON, DC

■■■ Children from St. Raphael's School in Rockville, Md., await Pope Benedict XVI's arrival
at the Apostolic Nunciature (Vatican Embassy) in Washington, DC on April 15.
© MICHAEL HOYT, CATHOLIC STANDARD NEWSPAPER, WASHINGTON, DC

■■■ Pope Benedict XVI waves to the cheering crowd after his arrival
at the Apostolic Nunciature (Vatican Embassy) in Washington, DC
on April 15. Standing next to him is Archbishop Pietro Sambi,
the Apostolic Nuncio to the United States.
© MICHAEL HOYT, CATHOLIC STANDARD NEWSPAPER, WASHINGTON, DC

Apostolic Nunciature

While visiting Washington, DC, Pope Benedict re-
sided at the Apostolic Nunciature, the residence of the
apostolic nuncio to the United States, on Massachusetts
Avenue in Northwest Washington. This historic Art Deco
building stands near the Naval Observatory, the residence
of the vice president of the United States. The apostolic
nuncio represents the Holy See to the government of the
United States. In this diplomatic aspect, the nunciature is
an embassy. However, the nuncio also serves as a liaison
between the Holy See and the USCCB and takes an active
role in the selection and appointment of bishops in the
United States.

- Reception on the South Lawn of the White House -

Washington, DC
Wednesday, April 16th
10:30 a.m.

Before the Holy Father left the Nunciature for 1600 Pennsylvania Avenue, large crowds had already gathered on the South Lawn, surrounded by the colors of flags, uniforms, and yellow and white tulips. In what the media reported as the largest gathering in recent White House history, more than 12,000 people awaited Pope Benedict in a festive atmosphere punctuated by music and the arrival of dignitaries. A Knights of Columbus honor guard led a procession onto the lawn that included Vice President Dick Cheney, members of Congress, a number of prelates, as well as Boy Scouts and Girl Scouts.

■■■ Children from nearby Annunciation School in Washington, DC wave flags as they stand outside the Apostolic Nunciature, where Pope Benedict XVI stayed during his April 15-17 visit to Washington, DC. The Pope greeted the children on April 16, the morning of his 81st birthday, and they sang "Happy Birthday" in German and in English.
© MICHAEL HOYT, CATHOLIC STANDARD NEWSPAPER, WASHINGTON, DC

■■■ School children singing "Happy Birthday" to Pope Benedict XVI.
© MICHAEL HOYT, CATHOLIC STANDARD NEWSPAPER, WASHINGTON, DC

■■■ A boy holds a birthday card for Pope Benedict XVI as he waits outside the Apostolic Nunciature in Washington, DC on April 16, the Pope's 81st birthday.
© MICHAEL HOYT, CATHOLIC STANDARD NEWSPAPER, WASHINGTON, DC

■■■ On the morning of April 16, his 81ˢᵗ birthday, Pope Benedict XVI appears in the doorway of the Apostolic Nunciature to greet and thank students from Annunciation School in Washington, DC who had serenaded him by singing "Happy Birthday" in German and in English. The Holy Father stayed at the nunciature during his visit to Washington, DC. At left is Archbishop Pietro Sambi, the Apostolic Nuncio to the United States, and at right is Washington Archbishop Donald Wuerl, the Pope's hosts in Washington. In a tour of the nunciature for reporters on the day before the Pope arrived, Archbishop Sambi showed them the small, ornate chapel where the Holy Father would be celebrating Mass on the morning of April 16 with members of the nunciature staff. "We will be his family on his birthday," Archbishop Sambi said.
© MICHAEL HOYT, CATHOLIC STANDARD NEWSPAPER, WASHINGTON, DC

■■■ Pope Benedict XVI thanks Denyce Daniels, center, the music teacher and choir director for Annunciation School in Washington, DC, and her students for singing to him on April 16, the morning of his birthday. The Pope was serenaded by the students outside the Apostolic Nunciature, which is about a mile and one-half from the school. The school's students can be seen at left, and the principal, Marguerite Conley, and the pastor, Msgr. V. James Lockman, are at center in the background.
© MICHAEL HOYT, CATHOLIC STANDARD NEWSPAPER, WASHINGTON, DC

■■■ Outside the Apostolic Nunciature on April 16, Pope Benedict XVI greets James Henkels, a student from St. Joseph's School in Vancouver, Wash., who like the Pope was celebrating his birthday that day. Henkels turned 11, while the Holy Father marked his 81ˢᵗ birthday.
© MICHAEL HOYT, CATHOLIC STANDARD NEWSPAPER, WASHINGTON, DC

I come as a friend, a preacher of the Gospel... with great respect for this vast pluralistic society.

The limousine carrying the Holy Father arrived at the South Lawn to the sounds of a drum roll and a trumpet flourish. President and Mrs. Bush stepped forward to greet His Holiness as he emerged from the car. Despite the many onlookers and the ceremony of the event, the Pontiff's arrival was simple and warm. He greeted the vice president and the congressional leadership before ascending the dais with the president. Pope Benedict and President Bush stood respectfully for the anthems of the Holy See and the United States while a 21-gun salute sounded from the Ellipse. The soprano Kathleen Battle then offered a moving rendition of the Lord's Prayer. A delightful moment took place when a marching drum and fife band in colonial dress ended its program with "Yankee Doodle Dandy." In the moments after the song, the crowds could not resist calling out their own spontaneous words of welcome and began a heartfelt, if off-key, singing of "Happy Birthday!"

■■■ Pope Benedict XVI arriving at the White House on April 16 is greeted by President George W. Bush and First Lady Laura Bush.
© RAFAEL CRISOSTOMO, CATHOLIC STANDARD NEWSPAPER, WASHINGTON, DC

President Bush's words of welcome to the Holy Father began with the traditional Christian greeting: *"pax tecum"* (peace be with you). The President went on to express his and the nation's gratitude for the Holy Father's pastoral visit. He spoke of America's deep religious faith and its best values, including compassion and the willingness to welcome religious perspectives in the public square. He praised Pope Benedict's personal example of faith, his message of hope and love, and the importance of his moral voice. To much applause, the president also affirmed America's need to hear the Holy Father's message of the dignity of human life:

In a world where some treat life as something to be debased and discarded, we need your message that all human life is sacred, and that 'each of us is willed, each of us is loved'...

Next, the Holy Father spoke with great serenity in English colored by his German accent. In his brief remarks, Pope Benedict described the character of his journey to the United States: *"I come as a friend, a preacher of the Gospel... with great respect for this vast pluralistic society."* He also expressed his wish that his visit serve as *"a source of renewal and hope for the Church in the United States."* He went on to praise the religious principles that *"forged the soul of a nation."*

Praising the liberty that characterizes American society, especially religious liberty, he reminded Americans that the gift of freedom comes with great responsibility:

The preservation of freedom calls for the cultivation of virtue, self-discipline, sacrifice for the common good and a sense of responsibility towards the less fortunate. It also demands the courage to engage in civic life and to bring one's deepest beliefs and values to reasoned public debate. In a word, freedom is ever new. It is a challenge held out to each generation, and it must constantly be won over for the cause of good.

Pope Benedict XVI and President George W. ■■■ Bush wave to the crowd of 13,000 people on the South Lawn of the White House April 16 for the ceremony welcoming the Pope on his first pastoral visit to the United States.
© RAFAEL CRISOSTOMO, CATHOLIC STANDARD NEWSPAPER, WASHINGTON, DC

■■■ Pope Benedict XVI and President George W. Bush stand on stage at the April 16 White House ceremony welcoming the Holy Father for his first pastoral visit to the United States.
© RAFAEL CRISOSTOMO, CATHOLIC STANDARD NEWSPAPER, WASHINGTON, DC

■■■ Pope Benedict XVI speaks during a White House ceremony.
© RAFAEL CRISOSTOMO, CATHOLIC STANDARD NEWSPAPER WASHINGTON, DC

■■■ Pope Benedict XVI and President Bush shake hands during the April 16 White House ceremony.
© RAFAEL CRISOSTOMO, CATHOLIC STANDARD NEWSPAPER, WASHINGTON, DC

■■■ Washington Archbishop Donald Wuerl, center, applauds
during the April 16 welcoming ceremony at the White House.
Standing among the cardinals, archbishops and bishops at the
ceremony are, at the far left Cardinal Tarcisio Bertone,
the Vatican's Secretary of State, and at far right Cardinal
Edward Egan of New York.

© RAFAEL CRISOSTOMO, CATHOLIC STANDARD NEWSPAPER, WASHINGTON, DC

The Previous Papal Visit to the White House

As the official residence of the president of the United
States, the White House has hosted numerous visiting
heads of state in its 200-year history. However, Pope
Benedict's visit to 1600 Pennsylvania Avenue marked
only the second time the leader of the world's smallest
sovereign state, the Holy See, has crossed the threshold of
this prestigious address. The previous papal visit occurred
on October 6, 1979, during Pope John Paul II's first trip to
the United States. After President Jimmy Carter welcomed
the Holy Father with a few words in Polish, the leaders
exchanged formal greetings and retired to the Oval Office for an hour-long private conversation. Significantly,
at the start of their meeting the Pontiff and President
Carter opted to speak as "Christian brothers" rather than
as diplomats. Their mutual commitment to promoting human rights weighed heavily in the conversation.

Invoking the words of George Washington's Farewell Address, which affirmed the importance of religion and morality in public life, the Pope appealed to Americans to apply the truth and wisdom of moral principles to national decisions in order to assure the flourishing of democracy. Pope Benedict ended his remarks with an enthusiastic and crowd-pleasing *"God bless America!"*

Following the Holy Father's remarks, President Bush thanked him for his *"awesome"* message. After the Army Chorus sang the "Battle Hymn of the Republic," the Pontiff accompanied President Bush to the portico of the White House, stopping for a now official singing of "Happy Birthday." Inside, the White House staff was ready with an impressive birthday cake. Pope Benedict concluded his visit with a forty-five minute private meeting with President Bush in the Oval Office.

For only the second time in history, a pope met at the White House with a president of the United States. There were many moments of great beauty amidst the joy of welcoming a friend. Above all, the papal visit provided an opportunity for significant and profound dialogue about the role of faith in society and governance.

Pope Benedict XVI acknowledges guests Wednesday, April 16, ■■■ 2008, during the arrival ceremony for the Pope on the South Lawn of the White House. Said Pope Benedict XVI during the ceremony, "Mr. President, dear friends, as I begin my visit to the United States, I express once more my gratitude for your invitation, my joy to be in your midst, and my fervent prayers that Almighty God will confirm this nation and its people in the ways of justice, prosperity and peace."
© DAVID BOHRER

■■■ President George W. Bush and Pope Benedict XVI look out onto the Rose Garden from the Colonnade of the White House before their meeting Wednesday, April 16, 2008. The visit of Pope Benedict XVI is the first White House papal visit in three decades.
© DAVID BOHRER

■■■ President George W. Bush and Mrs. Laura Bush stand with Pope Benedict XVI as he acknowledges the cheers from the crowd from the South Portico balcony Wednesday, April 16, 2008, on the South Lawn of the White House.
© GRANT MILLER

President George W. Bush and Laura Bush applaud as Pope Benedict XVI ■■■ acknowledges being sung happy birthday by the thousands of guests Wednesday, April 16, 2008, at his welcoming ceremony on the South Lawn of the White House.
© ERIC DRAPER

■■■ President George W. Bush and Mrs. Laura Bush lead the celebration of the 81ˢᵗ birthday of Pope Benedict XVI as he's presented a cake by White House Pastry Chef Bill Yosses Wednesday, April 16, 2008, at the White House.
© ERIC DRAPER

President George W. Bush and Laura Bush wave goodbye to Pope Benedict XVI as he prepares to leave the White House ■■■ Wednesday, April 16, 2008 in the Popemobile, following his official welcome to the White House.
© ERIC DRAPER

- Evening Prayer and Meeting with the Bishops at the National Shrine -

Washington, DC
Wednesday, April 16th
5:00 p.m.

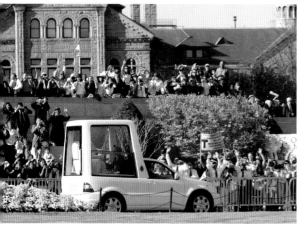

After returning to the Nunciature, the Holy Father attended a luncheon with the cardinals of the United States and leaders of the USCCB hosted by Archbishop Sambi. Later in the afternoon, before departing for his meeting with the bishops of the United States at the National Shrine of the Basilica of the Immaculate Conception, the Holy Father greeted the leaders of several Catholic charitable organizations.

■■■ Pope Benedict XVI arrives by Popemobile at the Basilica of the National Shrine of the Immaculate Conception in Washington, DC for a vespers service with U.S. bishops.
© CNS PHOTO/RICK MUSACCHIO

Women religious in the crowd cheer as Pope Benedict XVI waves from ■■■ the Popemobile while it passes by the Basilica of the National Shrine of the Immaculate Conception in Washington, DC on April 16.
© LESLIE KOSSOFF, CATHOLIC STANDARD NEWSPAPER, WASHINGTON, DC

■■■ Pope Benedict XVI waves from the Popemobile as it passes by the Basilica of the National Shrine of the Immaculate Conception on April 16.
© LESLIE KOSSOFF, CATHOLIC STANDARD NEWSPAPER, WASHINGTON, DC

■■■ Just after the Popemobile arrived on April 16 at the Basilica of the National Shrine of the Immaculate
Conception in Washington, DC, Pope Benedict XVI waves to the crowd. Behind him are Msgr. Walter Rossi,
the Rector of the National Shrine, and Washington Archbishop Donald Wuerl. They gave the Holy Father
a brief tour of the shrine before his evening prayer service there with the nation's Catholic bishops.

Upon arriving at the Basilica, the Holy Father, accompanied by Archbishop Donald Wuerl, exited the Popemobile and was welcomed by Msgr. Walter Rossi, the Shrine Rector. Before entering the Great Upper Church, the Holy Father waved to a large crowd of the faithful gathered outside. He then walked down the center aisle to the main altar. The Pontiff acknowledged the enthusiastic applause of the invited guests, gave his blessing, and proceeded to the Blessed Sacrament Chapel where he knelt for a period of private prayer. Leaving the chapel, he paused in the sanctuary as Archbishop Wuerl and Msgr. Rossi highlighted the new interior mosaics of the Incarnation and Redemption domes. He was then led to the Oratory of Our Lady of Altötting, a popular Marian shrine in his native Bavaria, where he again knelt for a short prayer.

Next, Pope Benedict was escorted to the Crypt Church. There he led the bishops of the United States in Solemn Vespers, which began with the Basilica Choir singing *Tu es Petrus*. After this celebration of Evening Prayer, the Pope returned to the chapel to address the more than 300 assembled bishops.

Seated in the center of the sanctuary His Holiness was flanked by Cardinal Tarcisio Bertone, the Secretary of State of the Holy See, and Cardinal Francis George, who welcomed the Pope *"not as a foreign visitor but as a father and friend in Christ."*

Pope Benedict XVI visits the Basilica of the ■■■ National Shrine of the Immaculate Conception to meet with U.S. bishops. Walking with the pontiff are Archbishop Donald Wuerl, second from left, and Msgr. Walter R. Rossi, Rector of the Basilica.
© CNS PHOTO/NANCY WIECHEC

I believe that the Church in America, at this point in her history, is faced with the challenge of recapturing the Catholic vision of reality and presenting it, in an engaging and imaginative way, to a society which markets any number of recipes for human fulfillment.

■■■ The Pope prays in the chapel of the Blessed Sacrament in the Basilica of the National Shrine of the Immaculate Conception.
© CNS PHOTO/KAREN CALLAWAY

■■■ The Pope is escorted by Msgr. Walter R. Rossi, Rector of the Basilica of the National Shrine, and Archbishop Donald W. Wuerl of Washington, to the upper church.
© CNS PHOTO/PAUL HARING

■■■ Pope Benedict XVI prays in a small alcove dedicated to Our Lady of Altotting at the Basilica of the National Shrine of the Immaculate Conception.
© CNS PHOTO/NANCY WIECHEC

■■■ Pope Benedict XVI stands in the upper church of the Basilica of the National Shrine of the Immaculate Conception before a vespers service with the U.S. bishops.
© CNS PHOTO/BOB ROLLER

■■■ Pope Benedict XVI arrives for prayer service with the U.S. bishops. ■■■
© CNS PHOTO/PAUL HARING

Basilica of the National Shrine of the Immaculate Conception

The Basilica of the National Shrine of the Immaculate Conception is the largest Catholic church in the United States. In 1920, Cardinal James Gibbons, the Archbishop of Baltimore, blessed the cornerstone. On Easter Sunday, 1924, the first Mass was celebrated. Construction on the Crypt Church was completed in 1926. The Great Depression and World War II delayed the construction of the Upper Church; it was resumed in the Marian Year of 1954 and dedicated on November 20, 1959. Work on the interior has continued since 1959. Archbishop Donald Wuerl presided over the dedications of the most recent additions, the Redemption Dome in 2006 and the Knights of Columbus Incarnation Dome in 2007.

Byzantine-Romanesque in architectural style, the artwork in the Shrine represents a unique American interpretation of biblical themes. The many chapels and oratories reflect the history of the Catholic experience in the United States, especially the central place of the Blessed Virgin Mary in the cultures and devotions of the various immigrant groups. Some of the chapels dedicated to her include: Our Mother of Africa, Our Lady of La Vang (Vietnam), Our Lady of China, Our Lady of Czestochowa (Poland), Our Lady of Guadalupe (Mexico), Mary Queen of Ireland, and Our Lady of Altötting (Germany).

On October 7, 1979, Pope John Paul II visited the National Shrine.

The Holy Father began his Address by recognizing the unique qualities of the Church in the United States. He lauded the unfailing generosity of the Church on both the national and the international level and expressed special thanks for the work of Catholic Charities. He also recognized the ongoing role of immigrants in American history, and noted their attraction to the country because of a profound *"respect for freedom of religion... deeply ingrained in the American consciousness."*

The heart of the Pontiff's Address was an exploration of how the 21st century bishop might lead the faithful to an encounter with Christ our hope. He first engaged the question by highlighting certain obstacles to faith today: secularism, materialism, and individualism. To the barrier of secularism, the Holy Father held up the transformative power of a faith that permeates one's entire life. In order to overcome the barrier of materialism, he stressed that the faithful *"need to be given opportunities to drink from the wells of his [God's] infinite love."* Finally, regarding the barrier of individualism, he underscored the Church's identity as a *"redeemed community"* called to evangelize culture.

Pope Benedict then challenged the bishops to form the hearts of a culturally diverse American laity. He also reminded them of their obligation *"to participate in the exchange of ideas in the public square"* and to ensure a proper formation of the faithful so that they might be authentic witnesses of the Gospel of life. He went on to stress the importance of family life, rooted in the lifelong commitment of a man and a woman in the institution of marriage, as giving such a witness. Seeing the family as *"the primary place for evangelization,"* the Pope recalled the importance of the domestic church in transmitting the faith.

Turning to the sensitive issue of the sexual abuse of minors, the Holy Father highlighted the *"compassion and care"* shown to the victims and noted the pain suffered and shame felt by the Church in confronting such *"gravely immoral behavior."* Speaking directly to the bishops, he reminded them that:

It is your God-given responsibility as pastors to bind up the wounds caused by every breach of trust, to foster healing, to promote reconciliation and to reach out with loving concern to those so seriously wronged.

In addition, he urged that the *"scourge"* of abuse be met with a *"determined, collective response"* and treated in the *"wider context"* of a *"moral renewal"* within society:

It falls to you, as pastors modeled upon Christ, the Good Shepherd, to proclaim this message loud and clear, and thus to address the sin of abuse within the wider context of sexual mores.

At the conclusion of his Address, the Holy Father stressed the importance of a life of prayer centered on Eucharistic Adoration, the Rosary, and the Liturgy of the Hours.

Following his formal remarks, the Pope took three questions from the American hierarchy. He responded to the question of Bishop J. Vann Johnston Jr. of the Diocese Springfield-Cape Girardeau in Missouri concerning the challenge of secularism and relativism by calling on American Catholics to recapture *"the Catholic vision of reality…in an engaging and imaginative way."* Archbishop Daniel Pilarczyk of Cincinnati raised a question regarding Catholics who have gradually distanced themselves from the Church through a lack of practice. After recognizing the complexity of the issue, Pope Benedict raised the possibility of inadequate preaching and teaching as a factor in this sad phenomenon, asking: *"Has our preaching lost its salt?"* Archbishop Basil Schott of the Archeparchy of Pittsburgh for Byzantines asked the Holy Father to share his thoughts on the issue of priestly vocations. In his response, the Pontiff addressed three areas. Regarding efforts to increase vocations, the Pope stressed the importance of prayer. Concerning those who have already responded to the call of Christ, the Holy Father focused on the need for sound formation in order for them to persevere. Finally, addressing those who have been ordained, His Holiness underscored the need for strong priestly fraternity, especially among younger clergy.

At the end of the Address, Cardinal George presented the Holy Father with a birthday gift of $870,000 from American Catholics to be distributed among the papal charities. The Pope then presented two gifts. He gave the Basilica Shrine the traditional gift of the "Golden Rose" in honor of Our Lady. This tradition, observed by popes since the Middle Ages, expressed the Holy Father's great reverence and affection for this National Shrine. As a sign of his *prayerful solidarity with the faithful of the Archdiocese of New Orleans,* so devastated by Hurricane Katrina, he presented Archbishop Alfred Hughes with a silver chalice. He left the chapel to the applause of the bishops and another chorus of "Happy Birthday," before returning to the nunciature.

■■■ The Pope greets U.S. bishops as he leaves a meeting with them at the Basilica of the National Shrine of the Immaculate Conception.
© CNS PHOTO/PAUL HARING

Pope Benedict XVI addresses U.S. bishops at the ■■■ Basilica of the National Shrine of the Immaculate Conception in Washington, DC. At right is Cardinal Francis E. George of Chicago, President of the U.S. Conference of Catholic Bishops.
© CNS PHOTO/PAUL HARING

Pope Benedict gives a gift of a chalice to Archbishop Alfred C. Hughes ■■■
of New Orleans at the Basilica of the National Shrine of the Immaculate Conception.
© CNS PHOTO/NANCY WIECHEC

31

April | 17

- Celebration of Holy Mass at Washington Nationals Park -

Washington, DC
Thursday, April 17th
10:00 a.m.

■■■ Knights of Columbus 4th Degree Color Guard
at Nationals Park, Washington, DC.
© COURTESY OF THE KNIGHTS OF COLUMBUS

On a beautiful spring morning, the Holy Father arrived at Washington's newest ballpark shortly after 9:30. He entered the stadium by Popemobile and was driven around the warning track. With the bulletproof windows down, he greeted the 46,000 people assembled for Mass while a choir of 600 men and women sang joyful hymns.

After vesting, the Pope, carrying his distinctive cruciform crozier previously used by Blessed Pope Pius IX in the 19th century, processed to the altar. He was joined in celebrating the Votive Mass of the Holy Spirit by fourteen cardinals, more than 250 bishops, and 1,300 priests. Archbishop Wuerl welcomed the Holy Father at the start of the Mass, describing the visit of *"our chief Shepherd and Vicar of Christ"* as a great blessing and *"a source of spiritual renewal."* He spoke of the roots of

POPE BENEDICT XVI APRIL 17, 2008 WASHINGTON DC

■■■ Pope Benedict XVI waves from the Popemobile as he enters Nationals Park to celebrate Mass in Washington, DC.
© CNS PHOTO/JOSHUA ROBERTS

Catholicism in nearby Maryland with the arrival of Catholics to St. Clements Island in 1634. From such humble beginnings, a Church has emerged with *"people from every continent and numerous cultural and ethnic backgrounds,"* a diversity displayed in those present for the Mass. His Excellency spoke for the entire gathering in welcoming the Pope as he leads Catholics in the effort to *"make all things new in Christ our hope."*

A special sanctuary had been constructed in centerfield with a large altar and furnishings designed by architecture students from The Catholic University of America. As has become the custom for Pope Benedict, a standing crucifix and seven large candlesticks were placed on the altar. In recognition of the multi-ethnic character of the Church in the United States, lectors proclaimed the readings in Spanish and English while the Prayer of the Faithful was offered in English, Spanish, Korean, Vietnamese, Tagalog, and Igbo. The wide variety of musical selections for the Mass included traditional Latin chant as well as contemporary compositions, particularly those of American composers. Especially moving was the solo rendition of *Panis Angelicus* by Placido Domingo. To the delight of Pope Benedict, Mozart's setting of *Ave Verum* was also performed.

In his first homily to Catholics in the United States, Pope Benedict called upon the faithful to open their hearts to the power of the Holy Spirit. He began by recalling the origins of the Church in *"the original Diocese of Baltimore and the establishment of the Dioceses of Boston, Bardstown (now Louisville), New York and Philadelphia."* Recognizing the rich history of the Church in America and the faith of previous generations, the Holy Father called Catholics today *"to look to the future"* so that·

■■■ Pope Benedict XVI waves to the crowd of 47,000 people at the new Nationals Park in Washington, DC on April 17 at his Papal Mass, his first public Mass as Pope in the United States.

© RAFAEL CRISOSTOMO, CATHOLIC STANDARD NEWSPAPER WASHINGTON, DC

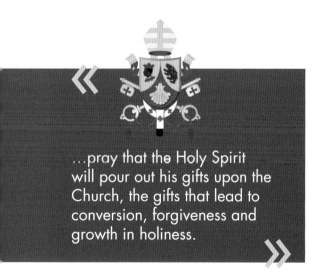

«

...pray that the Holy Spirit will pour out his gifts upon the Church, the gifts that lead to conversion, forgiveness and growth in holiness.

»

...this significant anniversary in the life of the Church in the United States, and the presence of the Successor of Peter in your midst, will be an occasion for all Catholics to reaffirm their unity in the apostolic faith, to offer their contemporaries a convincing account of the hope which inspires them (cf. 1 Pet 3:15), and to be renewed in missionary zeal for the extension of God's Kingdom.

According to the Holy Father, the realization of this hope for the future will come through *"sound instruction in the truths of the faith,"* and will blossom in:

...an intellectual "culture", which is genuinely Catholic, confident in the profound harmony of faith and reason, and prepared to bring the richness of faith's vision to bear on the urgent issues which affect the future of American society.

For the third consecutive day, Pope Benedict acknowledged the pain caused by the sexual abuse of minors. Having addressed the bishops the night before at the National Shrine, in this gathering he implored the laity *"to foster healing and reconciliation"* and *"to love your priests."* Most of all he called upon them to *"pray that the Holy Spirit will pour out his gifts upon the Church, the gifts that lead to conversion, forgiveness and growth in holiness."*

■■■ Attendees receive Communion at the April 17 Papal Mass at Nationals Park.
© MICHAEL HOYT, CATHOLIC STANDARD, WASHINGTON, DC

■■■ Members of the Intercultural Choir perform at Pope Benedict's April 17 Mass at Nationals Park in Washington, DC. The 65-voice Intercultural Choir included members from 35 countries singing in several languages, including French, Zulu and Spanish. The 570 singers in four different choirs practiced for months for the Papal Mass.
© MICHAEL HOYT, CATHOLIC STANDARD, WASHINGTON, DC

Shown on the large message screen at the new Nationals Park, ▪▪▪
Washington Archbishop Donald Wuerl welcomes Pope Benedict XVI
at the Papal Mass celebrated there on April 17.

▪▪▪ At the presentation of gifts, Pope Benedict XVI
receives the ciborium in the Offertory Procession
during the Papal Mass on April 17.

Members of the Intercultural Choir perform at ■■■
Pope Benedict's April 17 Mass at Nationals Park in
Washington, DC. The 65-voice Intercultural Choir is made up
of members from 35 countries singing in several languages,
including French, Zulu and Spanish.
© MICHAEL HOYT, CATHOLIC STANDARD

■■■ Pilgrims from St. Benedict the Moor Parish in Washington, DC
pray during the Papal Mass at Nationals Park on April 17.
© MICHAEL HOYT, CATHOLIC STANDARD

■■■ Members of the 250-voice Papal Mass Choir sing at Pope Benedict's April 17 Nationals Park Mass.
The 570 singers in four different choirs practiced for months for the Papal Mass.
© MICHAEL HOYT, CATHOLIC STANDARD

The Archdiocese of Washington DC

Catholic roots run deep in the region pertaining to the Archdiocese of Washington, DC. English Catholics seeking religious liberty founded Maryland, from which the Federal District was carved. In 1634, the first Mass was celebrated nearby on St. Clements Island. By the end of the 1600s, Maryland Catholics lost their religious liberty and had to await the American Revolution before they could once again worship in peace.

Because of these deep roots, Catholics have been present in Washington from its very inception. In 1789, one year before the creation of the Federal District, the Jesuits established Georgetown University on the Potomac River. By the 1790s, Irish laborers working to build the capital city established the first parish in the District, St. Patrick's.

Originally, Washington formed part of the first American Diocese, Baltimore. In 1939, in recognition of the growing size and importance of the Federal City, Pope Pius XII named Washington DC. an Archdiocese. Its location at the center of federal authority gives a unique character and a high profile to the See. It has accomplished pioneering pastoral work in key areas such as civil rights and outreach to immigrants. In addition to its many educational, pastoral, and charitable activities, the Archdiocese of Washington offers a Catholic voice and presence in the home of the nation's governing bodies.

Pope Benedict XVI appointed the current Archbishop, Most Reverend Donald Wuerl, in 2006. A native of Pittsburgh, Archbishop Wuerl is a nationally known catechist and author of the best-selling catechisms, *The Teaching of Christ* and *The Catholic Way*. His Excellency shepherds 580,000 Catholics in the District and five surrounding counties.

The Holy Father then urged the faithful to trust in the power of the Spirit, Who leads them to experience the freedom that comes from the grace of conversion. Specifically, he recommended a rediscovery of the sacrament of Penance for every Catholic, stressing that:

To a great extent, the renewal of the Church in America depends on the renewal of the practice of Penance and the growth in holiness which that sacrament both inspires and accomplishes.

The Pope concluded his homily with a greeting in Spanish which was received with great applause and cheers.

While the crowd was large and energetic, Pope Benedict's presence fostered a sense of serenity and solemnity throughout the Mass. In fact that very serenity characterized each of the events of the papal visit.

Pope Benedict XVI celebrates Mass at the new Nationals Park in ▪▪▪ Washington, DC. The altar and chair were designed by architecture students from The Catholic University of America, John-Paul Mikolajczyk and Ryan Mullen and completed by a carpenter who is a deacon in the archdiocese, Deacon Dave Cahoon.

© MICHAEL HOYT, CATHOLIC STANDARD, WASHINGTON, DC

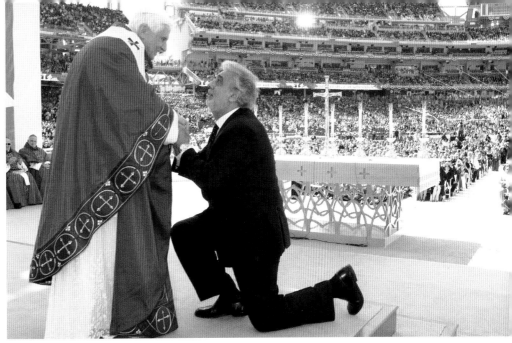

■■■ Opera star Placido Domingo sings «Panis Angelicus» after Communion during Pope Benedict XVI's Mass at Nationals Park

Placido Domingo kneeling before the Pope. ■■■■

■■■ Pope Benedict XVI acknowledges the crowd of 47,000 people at the new Nationals Park in Washington, DC on April 17 at his Papal Mass, his first public Mass in the United States as Pope.

- Address to Catholic Educators at The Catholic University of America -

Washington, DC
Thursday, April 17ᵗʰ
5:00 p.m.

Freedom is not an opting out. It is an opting in…

In a moment of great pastoral care, the Holy Father gathered with victims of clergy sexual abuse before departing for his scheduled Address at The Catholic University of America. Joined by the Archbishop of Boston, Cardinal Sean O'Malley, His Holiness prayed and conversed with the group in the chapel of the Apostolic Nunciature. He met with each of the victims individually, listened to their personal accounts, and offered words of encouragement and hope.

■■■ Pope Benedict XVI greets students at The Catholic University of America in Washington as he arrives for a meeting with Catholic educators. To his left is Vincentian Father David O'Connell, university president.
© GREG TARCZYNSKI

■■■ Catholic University of America freshmen Chris Anderson, Jeanette Teller, and Gabriell Reed cheer the arrival of Pope Benedict XVI to their school in Washington, DC.
© GREG TARCZYNSKI

The Catholic University of America

Founded by the bishops of the United States in 1887, The Catholic University of America enjoys a prominent location in Brookland in Northeast Washington, DC. Set in a neighborhood sometimes called "little Rome" because of the numerous houses of religious communities, the campus adjoins the National Shrine of the Immaculate Conception and the headquarters of the USCCB. With more than six thousand students, the university is unusual in that nearly half of them study at the graduate level. Established by papal charter in 1904, the graduate division of the university enjoys the right to grant pontifical degrees. The current president of the university is the Very Rev. David O'Connell, CM. The United States bishops continue to play an active role in the support and governance of this unique American and Catholic institution of higher learning.

Pope Benedict arrived at the university to a crowd of 4,000 students cheering *"Peter!"* and *"CUA loves the Pope!"* Upon exiting the limousine, the Holy Father was welcomed by Bishop William Lori of the Diocese of Bridgeport, Chairman of The Catholic University's Board of Trustees, and the University President, Rev. David O'Connell, CM. After entering the reception hall, Father O'Connell offered words of welcome before the Pontiff began his remarks to leaders in Catholic education at the grammar, secondary, and university levels.

The first part of the Address concerned the Church's mission to educate, an integral part of its obligation to preach the Good News. The Holy Father focused on the role of education in the life of the student as a way of developing a relationship with Jesus Christ that draws the student into a *"new life characterized by all that is beautiful, good, and true; a life of Christian witness…"* He stressed that while the call to educate belongs to the entire Christian community, Catholic educators have a special obligation *"to ensure that the power of God's truth permeates every dimension of the institution they serve."*

The Holy Father praised the tradition of Catholic education in the Unites States, calling it *"an outstanding apostolate of hope…"* He urged Catholics to contribute to, and so assure, the long-term sustainability of educational institutions.

He also reflected upon the unique contribution of the Church's work in education, a contribution rooted in Revelation and in the human desire for truth. The Catholicity of a school does not consist in the number of Catholic students but in the convictions of the educational community. These convictions find expression *"liturgically, sacramentally, through prayer, acts of charity, a concern for justice, and respect for God's creation."* The task of the Catholic school goes beyond the formation of the intellect to the formation of the will in the proper use of freedom: *"Freedom is not an opting out. It is an opting in… Hence authentic freedom can never be attained by turning away from God."*

Catholic education also makes important contributions to society at large, offering a foundation for human morality and ethics and reminding all that *"it is not praxis that creates truth but truth that should serve as the basis of praxis."* More than mere knowledge, truth *"leads us to discover the good."*

The Pope urged educators to dedicate themselves to *"intellectual charity,"* the recognition that *"the profound responsibility to lead the young to truth is nothing less than an act of love."* He also focused on the professionalism of educators and the quality of their witness as well as the accomplishments of Catholic educational institutions. He went on to affirm the value of academic freedom, but cautioned against appealing to principles of such freedom to *"justify positions that contradict the faith and the teaching of the Church."* This would betray the *"university's identity and mission…"* In fact, Catholic educators have the "duty and privilege" to ensure the instruction of their students in Catholic doctrine and practice.

The Holy Father concluded his remarks by praising catechists and religious men and women in educational apostolates, urging them to renew their commitment. Finally, he summed up his message to all of the educators:

Bear witness to hope. Nourish your witness with prayer. Account for the hope that characterizes your lives (cf. 1 Peter 3:15) by living the truth which you propose to your students.

After offering his Apostolic Blessing, Pope Benedict departed the hall to warm applause, stopping to greet numerous individuals.

■■■ Vincentian Father David M. O'Connell, President of The Catholic University of America, welcomes Pope Benedict XVI to a gathering of Catholic educators at the university in Washington, DC. Seated at left are Cardinal William J. Levada, head of the Vatican's Congregation for the Doctrine of the Faith; Cardinal Tarcisio Bertone, Vatican Secretary of State; and Washington Archbishop Donald W. Wuerl.
© CNS PHOTO/NANCY WIECHEC

- Meetings with Interreligious Leaders and Jewish Representatives -

John Paul II Cultural Center
Washington, DC
Thursday, April 17th
6:30 p.m.

■■■ Pope Benedict XVI attends an April 17 meeting with interreligious leaders at the Pope John Paul II Cultural Center in Washington, DC. He met with about 200 representatives of Islam, Jainism, Buddhism, Hinduism and Judaism.
© LESLIE KOSSOFF, CATHOLIC STANDARD NEWSPAPER, WASHINGTON, DC

Following his Address to the Catholic educators, the Holy Father traveled a short distance to meet with representatives of Judaism, Islam, Jainism, Buddhism and Hinduism at the John Paul II Cultural Center. Milwaukee Auxiliary Bishop Richard Sklba, Chairman of the USCCB Committee on Ecumenical and Interreligious Affairs, welcomed Pope Benedict and 200 invited guests.

The Pope praised the rich history of collaboration which has marked the religious diversity of the United States. He cited both the celebration of common national feasts and the search for *"mutual understanding"* on issues which *"promote the common good."* He extolled this American experience of religious diversity and collaboration as a model that could serve others.

As the handing on of vibrant religious traditions *"sustains and nourishes the surrounding culture,"* interreligious dialogue not only strengthens the bonds of mutual understanding, but serves society when it bears witness to common *"moral truths."* Bearing this in mind, Pope Benedict identified the grave responsibility of religious leaders:

> *...to imbue society with a profound awe and respect*
> *for human life and freedom;*
> *to ensure that human dignity is recognized and cherished;*
> *to facilitate peace and justice;*
> *to teach children what is right, good and reasonable!*

The Pope linked dialogue to the pursuit of, and discovery of, truth. Through dialogue we explore the deepest questions of the human heart concerning our origins, our purpose, and our final end. For Christians, these questions find their answer in Jesus, *"… the eternal Logos who became flesh in order to reconcile man to God and reveal the underlying reason of all things."*

Authentic dialogue also brings us to discover differences among ourselves. However, this should not discourage us:

We have no reason to fear, for the truth unveils for us the essential relationship between the world and God. We are able to perceive that peace is a "heavenly gift" that calls us to conform human history to the divine order…

In conclusion, Pope Benedict invited the religious leaders to view dialogue and the pursuit of the truth as a means whereby *"we can be instruments of peace for the whole human family."*

Pope Benedict XVI speaks during an April 17 ■■■ meeting with interreligious leaders at the Pope John Paul II Cultural Center in Washington, DC. He met with about 200 representatives of Islam, Jainism, Buddhism, Hinduism and Judaism.
© LESLIE KOSSOFF, CATHOLIC STANDARD NEWSPAPER, WASHINGTON, DC

…we can be instruments of peace for the whole human family.

■■■ At Pope Benedict XVI's April 17 meeting with interreligious leaders at the Pope John Paul II Cultural Center in Washington, DC the Catholic bishops included, from left to right, Archbishop Pietro Sambi, the Apostolic Nuncio to the United States; Cardinal James Francis Stafford, the Vatican's Major Penitentiary; Chicago Cardinal Francis George, President of the U.S. Conference of Catholic Bishops; and Washington Archbishop Donald Wuerl.
© LESLIE KOSSOFF, CATHOLIC STANDARD NEWSPAPER, WASHINGTON, DC

Pope John Paul II Cultural Center

In 1988, Pope John Paul II approved the proposal of then Bishop Adam Maida of Green Bay for a Catholic center in the nation's capital that would assist people in living their faith in today's world. To the delight of now Cardinal Maida, Archbishop of Detroit, the center opened in March 2001.

The mission of the Center is to explore the interaction between faith and culture. It uses interactive technology to foster such knowledge for all age groups. The Center highlights the life and legacy of Pope John Paul II whose spiritual, intellectual, pastoral, and diplomatic initiatives sought to promote the interaction between faith and culture. Finally, the Center is a place of scholarly research in matters of faith and culture, especially interreligious dialogue.

After the Pope's Address, Father James Massa, the Executive Director for the Secretariat for Ecumenical and Interreligious Affairs of the USCCB, brought forward five young representatives of the various religious groups to present the Holy Father with symbols from their own traditions: a Menorah from the Jewish community, a Qur'an from the Muslim community, a Jain metallic cube representing harmony, a Buddhist monastic bell, and a sculpture of the syllable "Om" which is sacred to Hindus.

At the conclusion of the ceremony, Pope Benedict met with a group of Jewish representatives in the Cultural Center's Polish Heritage Room where he extended his greetings to them on the occasion of their annual celebration of Passover. He used the occasion to express how *"our shared hope for peace in the world embraces the Middle East and the Holy Land in particular."*

Following his visit to the John Paul II Cultural Center, the Pope returned to the nunciature for his final night in Washington.

■■■ During an April 17 meeting with interreligious leaders at the Pope John Paul II Cultural Center in Washington, DC Pope Benedict XVI greets Saman Hussain, a young adult Muslim woman who presented him with a book of poetic verses from the Koran, the holy book of Islam.
© LESLIE KOSSOFF, CATHOLIC STANDARD NEWSPAPER, WASHINGTON, DC

■■■ During an April 17 meeting with interreligious leaders at the Pope John Paul II Cultural Center in Washington, DC Pope Benedict XVI receives a gift, including a metal bell, from Buddhist youth leader Masako Fukata. Bells are used to demarcate the times of meditation for Buddhists.
© LESLIE KOSSOFF, CATHOLIC STANDARD NEWSPAPER, WASHINGTON, DC

■■■ During an April 17 meeting with interreligious leaders at the Pope John Paul II Cultural Center in Washington, DC Pope Benedict XVI greets Bishop Jongmae Kenneth Park of the Korean Buddhist Taego Order.
© LESLIE KOSSOFF, CATHOLIC STANDARD NEWSPAPER, WASHINGTON, DC

■■■ During an April 17 meeting with interreligious leaders at the Pope John Paul II Cultural Center in Washington, DC Pope Benedict XVI greets a rabbi.
© LESLIE KOSSOFF, CATHOLIC STANDARD NEWSPAPER, WASHINGTON, DC

April | 18

- Arrival at John F. Kennedy International Airport -

Queens, NY
Friday, April 18th
9:30 a.m.

On Friday morning, the Holy Father arrived at John F. Kennedy Airport in the Diocese of Brooklyn. Cardinal Edward Egan of the Archdiocese of New York, Archbishop Celestino Migliore, the Holy See's Permanent Observer to the United Nations, Bishop Nicholas DiMarzio of Brooklyn, Thomas Daily, the Bishop emeritus of Brooklyn, Bishop William Murphy of the nearby Diocese of Rockville Centre, state and local officials, and various other dignitaries welcomed the Pope to New York. Two children from Catholic schools in the Diocese of Brooklyn presented Pope Benedict with flowers as onlookers called out their joy and welcome. A police honor guard stood at attention while a band played the Vatican Anthem. The Pope then boarded a Marine helicopter for the brief trip to the United Nations. While Pope Benedict was a passenger on the helicopter, he is certified to fly a helicopter and reportedly did so on at least one occasion as he traveled to the papal summer residence at Castelgandolfo.

The Diocese of Brooklyn

The turn of the 19th century saw the increased growth of the Catholic population on Long Island. In 1822, Peter Turner, who had emigrated from Ireland, organized the first Catholic society. On August 28, 1823, St. James, Long Island's first Catholic church, was consecrated. In 1853, Blessed Pope Pius IX created the Diocese of Brooklyn, establishing the geographical territory of Long Island as its own diocese.

The history of the Church on Long Island is the history of the Catholic immigrant experience. The Diocese of Brooklyn, composed of the counties of Kings and Queens, has the distinction of being both the smallest diocese in the United States geographically and the only totally urban diocese. The Diocese of Brooklyn is home to over 1.5 million Catholics from 167 countries. In the diocese, Mass is celebrated in twenty-six languages every week. In 1957, the Diocese of Rockville Centre was formed from the counties of Suffolk and Nassau.

On October 3, 2003, Bishop Nicholas DiMarzio was installed as the seventh Bishop of Brooklyn. Having served previously as the Bishop of Camden, New Jersey, Bishop DiMarzio is a recognized expert in matters affecting migrants and immigrants. In 2000, he was appointed a member of the Pontifical Council for the Pastoral Care of Migrants and Itinerant People.

■■■ The Brooklyn Bridge.
© ÉDITIONS DU SIGNE

- The Visit to the United Nations -

New York City
Friday, April 18th
10:30 a.m.

Located on the East side of Manhattan, the United Nations overlooks the East River on land designated international territory. As the Holy Father arrived at the United Nations, the crowds outside were particularly energetic, beating drums, chanting, and playing musical instruments. The joyful atmosphere continued inside as the Pontiff was received by the General Secretary of the United Nations, Ban Key-moon. After a private meeting with the General Secretary, the Holy Father entered the General Assembly to speak before the representatives of the member states. The Pope took his place on a large white chair near the rostrum and the President of the General Assembly, Dr. Srgjan Kerim, welcomed him, expressing the gratitude of the United Nations for the work of the Catholic Church and that of Pope Benedict himself. He concluded by assuring His Holiness that *"we count on your continued blessing and support as we pursue our work."*

Next, the General Secretary, Ban Key-moon, added his words of welcome. While acknowledging the secular character of the United Nations, he highlighted the religious motivations of so many of those who participate in its mission, and he told the Holy Father that *"in so many ways our mission unites us with yours."*

Pope Benedict began his remarks in French before switching to English for the last two-thirds of his Address. In the French language section, the Holy Father reaffirmed the foundational principles of the United Nations and cited the support for its work offered by his predecessors, Pope Paul VI and Pope John Paul II. The Pontiff added his own expressions of support

■■■ Pope Benedict XVI with Ban Ki-moon,
Secretary-General of the United Nations, right,
and Srgjan Kerim, President of the U.N.
General Assembly, at the United Nations.
© JOE VERICKER/PHOTOBUREAU

and esteem for the essential work of the General Assembly.
He expressed his conviction that the world is in ever more need
of collective action and dialogue in the face of the challenges
presented by conflict, poverty, inequality, environmental damage, and the effects of globalization. He spoke strongly of the
importance of the common good and the obligations of governments to protect and promote the true well being of their peoples.
In fact, the Pope asserted that the very legitimacy of governments
derives from their protection of the common good.

Citing the anniversary of the *United Nation's Universal Declaration of Human Rights*, Pope Benedict reminded the Assembly
that human rights do not derive from legislative enactments or the

Pope Benedict XVI with a children's orchestra ■■■
at the United Nations.
© MARIA R. BASTONE, CATHOLIC NEW YORK

decisions of authorities, rather *"they are based on the natural law inscribed on human hearts and present in different cultures and civilizations"* (translated from the French). The Holy Father also outlined the essential role of religious faith in maintaining human rights in a rapidly changing world:

...a vision of life firmly anchored in the religious dimension can help to achieve this, since recognition of the transcendent value of every man and woman favors conversion of heart, which then leads to a commitment to resist violence, terrorism and war, and to promote justice and peace.

«

...the Church is committed to contributing her experience 'of humanity'...

»

Papal Visits to the United Nations

Pope Paul VI was the first pope to visit the United Nations. He addressed the General Assembly on October 4, 1965 during the first papal trip to the United States. In his address he told the members that they formed *"a bridge between peoples,"* and he called on the organization to work for peace through the promotion of justice. His address is often remembered for his impassioned cry, *"Jamais la guerre!" Never again war!*

Pope John Paul II visited the United Nations during two of his visits to the United States. On October 2, 1979, he addressed the General Assembly and underlined *"the special bond of cooperation which links the Apostolic See with the United Nations Organization..."* This bond is especially evident in the defense and promotion of human rights around the world. On October 5, 1995, John Paul II again addressed the General Assembly on the occasion of the fiftieth anniversary of the world organization's foundation. He told his audience that he came before them *"as a witness... a witness to human dignity, a witness to hope..."* He concluded his address with the invitation to realize that the answer to the fear that marked human existence at the end of the 20th century *"... is the common effort to build the civilization of love..."* This civilization of love is to be formed in a *"culture of freedom,"* rooted in self-giving and solidarity.

■■■ Pope Benedict XVI delivers address to U.N. General Assembly.
© MARIA R. BASTONE, CATHOLIC NEW YORK

■■■ Pope Benedict XVI tours U.N. headquarters with Archbishop Celestino Migliore, Vatican Nuncio to the U.N. In background is Ban Ki-moon, U.N. Secretary-General.
© MARIA R. BASTONE, CATHOLIC NEW YORK

In addition to seeing the importance of religious voices in international dialogue, governments must also recognize the inviolability of religious liberty:

It is inconceivable, then, that believers should have to suppress a part of themselves –their faith– in order to be active citizens. It should never be necessary to deny God in order to enjoy one's rights.

The Holy Father warned against reducing religious liberty to mere freedom of worship. Especially concerned for people who live in a context of a *"prevailing secular ideology"* or *"majority religious positions of an exclusive nature,"* he called for the full and free participation of all believers in society. Such participation helps to build up the society and to prevent an overly individualistic approach that would *"fragment the unity of the person."*

Pope Benedict pledged the willingness of the Catholic Church to take part in building the common good of nations and individuals. The Church contributes her moral voice and the resources of the Holy See. This is particularly true in the General Assembly of the United Nations which:

… remains a privileged setting in which the Church is committed to contributing her experience 'of humanity', developed over the centuries among peoples of every race and culture, and placing it at the disposal of all members of the international community.

The Holy Father concluded by testifying that the fundamental motivation for the Church's role in the world is her *"hope drawn from the saving work of Jesus Christ."* After pronouncing a blessing in the five official languages of the United Nations, Pope Benedict left the rostrum to a standing ovation.

After the Address, the Pope exited with the General Secretary. Later, he addressed further remarks to the staff and personnel of the United Nations. In that Address, he praised and thanked them for their dedicated service and noted their many sacrifices, including those who have sacrificed their lives in the pursuit of peace.

Commenting on the contrast in scale between the small geographic area of Vatican City State and its global outreach and interests, the Holy Father noted a similar contrast at the United Nations whose international territory is tiny, but whose mission encompasses the planet. In the same vein, he observed that the art on display in both the Vatican and the United Nations helps to remind those who serve of their global mission.

At the conclusion of the Pope's visit to the United Nations, he returned to the residence of Archbishop Migliore.

Mission of the Holy See to the United Nations

The United Nations brings together the countries of the world for mutual understanding and dialogue and the promotion of peace and human rights. The presence of the Holy See at this international organization rests on the simple fact that it too is a sovereign state, although its role differs from that of other nations. With no political, military, or economic agenda, the Holy See, by its own choice, enjoys the status of Permanent Observer rather than that of full member and maintains absolute neutrality. Primarily, this means that the Church's delegation participates in discussions but refrains from voting on propositions. In its interventions, the Holy See offers the international body the moral and spiritual principles that should animate the life of nations and foster their relations. Archbishop Celestino Migliore has carried out this vital task of the Church since his appointment as Permanent Observer by Pope John Paul II in 2002.

■■■ A group from St. John Vianney parish, the Bronx, banner in hand, welcomes pontiff outside United Nations.
© MARIA R. BASTONE, CATHOLIC NEW YORK

- Visit to the Park East Synagogue -

New York City
Friday, April 18th
5:00 p.m.

On Friday evening, Pope Benedict became the first pope to visit a synagogue in America. As the Pope and his entourage entered the historic Park East Synagogue at East 67th Street on the Upper East Side of Manhattan, he was greeted and accompanied to his seat on the bema by Rabbi Arthur Schneier. During the visit, which occurred a day before the beginning of the Jewish Passover, children sang several songs in Hebrew. In his remarks, Rabbi Schneier recognized the historic occasion as a welcome opportunity for building a stronger relationship between Catholics and Jews. The rabbi also toasted Pope Benedict with a hearty *"mazel tov"* on the occasion of the Pope's recent birthday and in anticipation of the third anniversary of his election on April 19th as the 265th successor of St. Peter.

The Holy Father opened his remarks with the Hebrew word for peace, *"Shalom,"* and expressed his joy at being in the synagogue just hours before the beginning of the celebration of Passover. He reminded the congregation and invited guests that, *"Jesus, as a young boy, heard the words of Scripture and prayed in a place such as this."* He then urged all present *"to continue building bridges of friendship with all the many different ethnic and religious groups present in your neighborhood."*

At the end of the visit, Pope Benedict and Rabbi Schneier exchanged gifts. Rabbi Schneier gave the Pope a large Seder plate, while the His Holiness gave the rabbi a 15th century manuscript from the Vatican Library.

Pope Benedict XVI presents Rabbi Arthur Schneier of the Park East Synagogue with a replica ■■■
of a medieval Jewish manuscript from the Vatican library. It was the first time
a pope visited a synagogue in the United States.

– Ecumenical Encounter at
the Church of St. Joseph –

New York City
Friday, April 18ᵗʰ
6:00 p.m.

■■■ Crowd waves golden handkerchiefs outside St. Joseph's Church.
© EILEEN MILLER, CATHOLIC NEW YORK

Established in 1873 as a German national parish in the Yorkville section on the Upper East Side of Manhattan, St. Joseph's Roman Catholic Church provided the venue for the Holy Father's ecumenical prayer service with about 250 national and local leaders of Orthodox churches and Protestant communities in the United States.

In his Address, the Holy Father acknowledged *"the contribution of Christians in the United States"* to the worldwide ecumenical movement. He reminded those present that all disciples of Jesus have received a mandate to build up the Body of Christ. In this noble task they can be certain that they will never be abandoned by the Holy Spirit.

Pope Benedict, the life-long scholar and preeminent theologian, offered an in-depth analysis of the genuine challenges to ecumenical discourse. The contemporary phenomenon of globalization results both in a greater sense of our connections with one another, while at the same time many experience fragmentation in their lives. Secularism and advances in technology can threaten the credibility of a transcendent faith. Division among Christians themselves compromises the Gospel message for non-Christians. Beliefs that are at the creedal core of Christianity, *"are sometimes changed within communities by so-called 'prophetic actions' that are based on a hermeneutic not always consonant with the datum of Scripture and Tradition."*

■■■ St. Joseph's Church, Yorkville.
© ST. JOSEPH'S CHURCH

■■■ Pope Benedict XVI kisses baby before entering church as child's mother smiles.
© EILEEN MILLER, CATHOLIC NEW YORK

■■■ 11-year-old girl in homemade papal hat
behind barrier with her father
© EILEEN MILLER, CATHOLIC NEW YORK

«

...the unity of the
Church flows from the
perfect oneness of the
Trinitarian God.

»

Pope Benedict XVI stands next to Bishop ■■■
Dennis J. Sullivan, Vicar General of the Archdiocese
of New York, who delivered the welcome
at the ecumenical prayer service at
St. Joseph's Church in Yorkville.
© CHRIS SHERIDAN, CATHOLIC NEW YORK

In light of such challenges, His Holiness proposed that one must recognize that, *"the unity of the Church flows from the perfect oneness of the Trinitarian God."* The early Christian community knew *"that its unity was both caused by, and is reflective of, the unity of the Father, Son, and Holy Spirit."* The role of *"normative doctrine expressed in creedal formulae,"* preserved the unity of the Church. Therefore, any trace of philosophical relativism concerning Christian doctrine in attempts to heal the wounds in the Church will result in a false peace. Rather, our witness must *"be based upon the notion of normative apostolic teaching: a teaching which indeed underlies the inspired word of God and sustains the sacramental life of Christians today."*

Pope Benedict, a man of prayer and a pastor, concluded his remarks with an unambiguous affirmation of the central role of prayer in the ecumenical movement.

After the Pope's talk, Cardinal Edward Egan presented the various Orthodox and Protestant leaders to the Holy Father. Following the ecumenical prayer service, the Pontiff departed for dinner with the cardinals of the United States and the officers of the USCCB at the residence of the Holy See's Permanent Observer to the United Nations.

Outside the residence, close to 1,000 young adults gathered in prayer and vigil with drums and guitars. Notable in the crowd were young members of the Sisters of Life, Franciscan Friars of the Renewal, and Legionaries of Christ. After dinner, Pope Benedict surprised the gathering with an impromptu visit, greeting and speaking with the thrilled young people.

■■■ Close-up of nun having her candle lighted.
© ANTHONY PERROTTO, CATHOLIC NEW YORK

■■■ Young boy shares in the spirit of the gathering.
© ANTHONY PERROTTO, CATHOLIC NEW YORK

■■■ Large crowd sings during candlelight vigil.
© ANTHONY PERROTTO, CATHOLIC NEW YORK

April | 19

– Celebration of Holy Mass at St. Patrick's Cathedral with Clergy and Men and Women in Consecrated Life –

New York City
Saturday, April 19th
9:15 a.m.

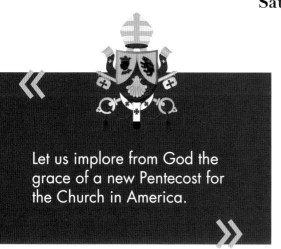

Let us implore from God the grace of a new Pentecost for the Church in America.

Outside New York City's famed St. Patrick's Cathedral, large crowds on Fifth Avenue awaited the Holy Father with great anticipation. Amidst their cheers and applause, the Rector of the Cathedral, Msgr. Robert Ritchie, welcomed the Pope. After waving to the crowds, Pope Benedict entered St. Patrick's vested in the distinctive white *mozzetta* traditionally worn by popes during the Easter season. At the entrance of the cathedral, the Pontiff was offered a crucifix to venerate. He blessed those gathered by the great bronze doors and then moved into the nave, greeting the exuberant congregation as the choir intoned the joyful hymn: *"Christus vincit, Christus regnat, Christus imperat"* (Christ conquers, Christ reigns, Christ rules over all). After a brief visit

■■■ Five students from Ave Maria University clap for the pope.
© EILEEN MILLER CATHOLIC NEW YORK

■■■ Pope Benedict XVI is greeted by Cardinal Egan and New York City Mayor Michael R. Bloomberg outside St. Patrick's Cathedral.
© JOE VERICKER/PHOTOBUREAU

before the Blessed Sacrament in the apse of the cathedral, Pope Benedict vested for the celebration of Mass.

He reentered the nave in a solemn procession. The choir and musicians accompanied the entrance with the beautiful hymn, "O God Beyond All Praising." The effect of the music, the joyful atmosphere, the colorful procession, and the beauty of the setting can only be described as mystical.

At the outset of the Mass, Cardinal Egan offered words of welcome to the Pontiff. He spoke of the importance of St. Patrick's as a *"beloved house of prayer"* which sees visitors of *"all faiths and cultures."* It is a great church built with the *"pennies of the poor"* in an archdiocese where Mass is celebrated each Sunday in thirty-five languages. The Cardinal commended the priests and religious present to the Holy Father, who knows their *"successes and defeats"* and who summons them to *"fulfill the vocation of hope,"* and he pledged the loyalty and love of all to the Pope. His Eminence concluded with warm congratulations to the Holy Father on the occasion of his third anniversary of election as the Supreme Pontiff.

Pope Benedict XVI on steps of St. Patrick's Cathedral before entering to celebrate Papal Mass. ■■■
With him are Msgr. Robert Ritchie, second from left, Rector of St. Patrick's, and Cardinal Edward Egan of New York, right.

■■■ Crowd reaching up to photograph the Pope as he arrives.

■■■ Bishops wave at nuns behind barrier.

■■■ Pope Benedict XVI blesses those gathered
at St. Patrick's Cathedral.
© JOE VERICKER/PHOTOBUREAU

In the homily, Pope Benedict acknowledged his joy in celebrating the Mass with the clergy and religious who:

… have been chosen by the Lord, who have answered his call, and who devote your [their] lives to the pursuit of holiness, the spread of the Gospel and the building up of the Church in faith, hope and love.

He also praised the *"countless men and women who have gone before us"* and *"left us a lasting legacy of faith and good works."* While giving thanks for these blessings, the Holy Father also implored God for *"the grace of a new Pentecost for the Church in America."*

■■■ The congregation inside St. Patrick's Cathedral
reacts to presence of the Holy Father.
© JOE VERICKER/PHOTOBUREAU

Pope Benedict XVI is accompanied by Cardinal Egan and ■■■
several members of the Vatican entourage at Lady Chapel.
© CHRIS LAPUTT, CATHOLIC NEW YORK

Like his predecessor Pope John Paul II, Pope Benedict asserted the task of the Church *"to proclaim the gift of life, to serve life, and to promote a culture of life."* This proclamation of life in abundance, a task *"at the heart of the new evangelization,"* is urgent and difficult in a world where self-centeredness and cynicism *"often choke the fragile growth of grace in people's hearts."* Further, this choice for life can be lost sight of *"in a society where the Church seems legalistic and 'institutional' to many people."* The challenge for believers is *"to communicate the joy born of faith and the experience of God's love."*

In the body of his homily, the Holy Father invoked the imagery and Gothic architecture of St. Patrick's Cathedral, which the 19th century Archbishop of New York, John Hughes, hoped would *"remind the young Church in America of the great spiritual tradition to which it was heir, and to inspire it to bring the best of that heritage to the building up of Christ's body in this land."* Pope Benedict's first illustration employed the beautiful stained glass windows of the cathedral. To the observer on the outside, they appear dreary, but within the church these same windows come alive as the light passes through them and reveals their splendor. Likewise, the true understanding of the mystery of the Church must come from within:

■■■ Holy Father wears the distinctive mozzetta, traditionally worn by popes during the Easter season.
© CHRIS LAPUTT, CATHOLIC NEW YORK

It is only from the inside, from the experience of faith and ecclesial life, that we see the Church as she truly is: flooded with grace, resplendent in beauty, adorned by the manifold gifts of the Spirit.

The homily devoted a great deal of attention to the importance of healing division and promoting unity within the Church. Noting that the experience of division has compromised the Second Vatican Council's renewed mission to the world, the Holy Father called for unity in Christ: *"We can only move forward if we turn our gaze together to Christ!"*

■■■ The cathedral's architecture is in view as congregation starts to arrive for Papal Mass.
© CHRIS LAPUTT, CATHOLIC NEW YORK

■■■ The Pope presents Book of the Gospels to deacon at Papal Mass.

Bishops are in alignment at Papal Mass. ■■■

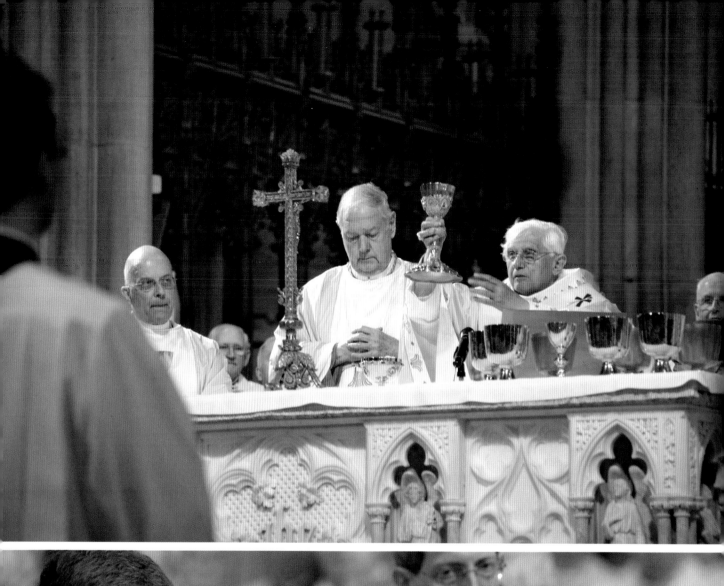

Pope Benedict characterized such unity, manifested in faith, conversion, and self-sacrifice, as the *"secret of the impressive growth of the Church"* in the United States. He cited the examples of Venerable Father Michael McGivney, the 19th century priest who founded the Knights of Columbus, and generations of priests and religious *"who quietly devoted their lives to serving the People of God in countless schools, hospitals and parishes."*

Having spoken on previous occasions to the bishops of the United States and the faithful about the pain caused by the sexual abuse of minors, the Pope now addressed the issue with the clergy and religious, assuring the gathering of his personal solidarity with them:

Here I simply wish to assure you, dear priests and religious, of my spiritual closeness as you strive to respond with Christian hope to the continuing challenges that this situation presents. I join you in praying that this will be a time of purification for each and every particular Church and religious community, and a time for healing.

He went on to express his hope that *"Our Lord Jesus Christ grant the Church in America a renewed sense of unity and purpose."*

We can only move forward if we turn our gaze together to Christ!

■■■ Group of clergy members seated in the cathedral
© MARIA R. BASTONE. CATHOLIC NEW YORK

■■■ Pope Benedict XVI acknowledges the applause of priests, deacons and religious who filled St. Patrick's Cathedral for the Papal Mass. With the Holy Father are, from left, Msgr. Konrad Krajewski, Assistant Papal Master of Ceremonies, and Msgr. Guido Marini, Papal Master of Ceremonies. © JOE VERICKER/PHOTOBUREAU

The Archdiocese of New York

The year 2008 marks the bicentennial celebration of the establishment of the Diocese of New York.

In 1643, St. Isaac Jogues, the French Jesuit missionary and martyr, found two Catholics in New York City as he traveled through on his way to France. By the time New York City served as the national capital (1789-1790), a small Catholic community had developed in the region. In 1808, Pope Pius VII created the Diocese of New York. Its boundaries included the entire state of New York and the northern portion of New Jersey. The Catholic population grew rapidly in the 19th century with the arrival of millions of immigrants from Europe. In 1850, Blessed Pope Pius IX elevated New York to an archdiocese. A symbol of the growing importance of the Catholic population in the city, St. Patrick's Cathedral was dedicated in 1879.

The 20th century and the opening of the 21st century have seen a vibrant Catholicism in the city that some have called the "capital of the world." The dedication of religious communities of women and men, the faith-filled generosity and entrepreneurial initiatives of members of the lay faithful, and strong leadership from the priests, bishops, and cardinal-archbishops have contributed to this vibrancy and growth in the Church in New York. The current Catholic population is estimated at more than 2.5 million, living in three of New York City's five boroughs, Manhattan, the Bronx, and Richmond, and in seven suburban counties.

A native of the Archdiocese of Chicago, a veteran of the Roman Curia, a judge of the Tribunal of the Sacred Roman Rota, and a noted canonist, Cardinal Egan assisted in the review of the new *Code of Canon Law* before its promulgation in 1983. Ordained a bishop in 1985, His Eminence served as Auxiliary Bishop and Vicar for Education of the Archdiocese of New York from 1985-1988 before his appointment as the Bishop of Bridgeport, Connecticut. Cardinal Edward Egan has served as the Archbishop of New York since his appointment in 2000 by Pope John Paul II, who elevated him to the College of Cardinals in 2001. Apart from his many administrative duties in Rome and in the Archdiocese, the Cardinal has made it a pastoral priority to visit a different parish each Sunday for Mass.

The Holy Father once again used the very architecture around him to make a point about unity and diversity. The Gothic structure contains diverse forces in dynamic tension, but achieves a fundamental unity and a common purpose in directing the pilgrim Church towards heaven. This common purpose is served by the universal call to holiness which becomes particular in the circumstances of individuals and their state in life. Pope Benedict expressed this in his reflection on the charisms proper to each clerical or religious vocation:

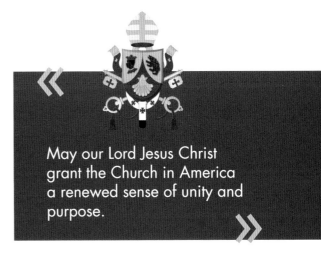

May our Lord Jesus Christ grant the Church in America a renewed sense of unity and purpose.

You, dear priests, by sacramental ordination have been configured to Christ, the Head of the Body. You, dear deacons, have been ordained for the service of that Body. You, dear men and women religious, both contemplative and apostolic, have devoted your lives to following the divine Master in generous love and complete devotion to his Gospel. All of you, who fill this cathedral today, as well as your retired, elderly and infirm brothers and sisters, who unite their prayers and sacrifices to your labors, are called to be forces of unity within Christ's Body.

Close-up of Pope Benedict XVI at Mass ■■■ in St. Patrick's Cathedral.
© JOE VERICKER/PHOTOBUREAU

He continued by exhorting those present to seek authenticity in their service, to grow in holiness, and to offer joyful witness, especially in befriending *"the poor, the homeless, the stranger, the sick and all who suffer."*

Having emphasized the beauty and impact of the cathedral in the course of his homily, the Pontiff concluded by pointing to the witness of the building itself in the midst of the city:

The spires of Saint Patrick's Cathedral are dwarfed by the skyscrapers of the Manhattan skyline, yet in the heart of this busy metropolis, they are a vivid reminder of the constant yearning of the human spirit to rise to God.

After the homily, the Mass continued with great solemnity and magnificent music and singing. Following the distribution of Holy Communion, Cardinal Bertone addressed the Holy

Father in Spanish, congratulating Pope Benedict on the anniversary of his election. The extended applause which followed elicited from Pope Benedict extemporaneous remarks. Calling himself *"a poor successor of St. Peter,"* he identified with Peter, who, for all his faults, was and is a *"rock for the Church."* His Holiness expressed his gratitude for the love which he received on the occasion, asked for prayers, and offered those assembled the gift of his Apostolic Blessing.

After Mass, the Holy Father joined Cardinal Egan and the bishops of New York State for lunch in the Cardinal's residence. Later in the afternoon, he traveled up Fifth Avenue in the Popemobile to the residence of Archbishop Migliore. Large crowds lined the route, cheering, singing, and calling out greetings to Pope Benedict.

Large crowds look on. ■■■

Papal watchers lined up from near ■■■
and far along Fifth Avenue, including
this group from California.

People extended as far as the eye could see ■■■
sought a glimpse of the pope after Papal Mass
at St. Patrick's Cathedral.

A group from the annual German-American ■■■
Steuben Parade poses near East 68th Street.

Exterior view of St. Patrick's Cathedral, ■■■
with Popemobile passing by on its way up
Fifth Avenue to residence of the Vatican
Nuncio.

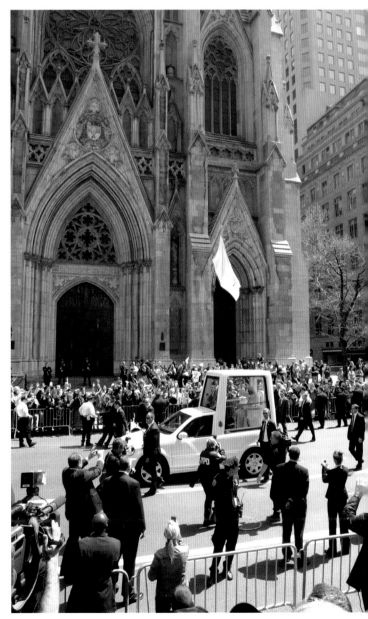

– Blessing of Youth with Disabilities at St. Joseph's Seminary –

Yonkers, NY
Saturday, April 19th
4:30 p.m.

St. Joseph's Seminary

Located in the Dunwoodie section of the City of Yonkers, fifteen miles north of Midtown Manhattan, St. Joseph's Seminary has formed priests for the Archdiocese of New York and areas beyond for over one hundred years. After efforts to establish a seminary in other parts of the Archdiocese, Archbishop Michael Corrigan laid the cornerstone of the present building in 1891. Since the magnificent structure opened in September 1896, it has enjoyed great respect. The Chapel of Saints Peter and Paul at the heart of the seminary has hosted one other Successor of Peter before Pope Benedict: Pope John Paul II, who visited on October 6, 1995 and addressed the faculty and seminarians during Vespers. Today, additional other buildings dot the seminary's 40 acres, including the St. John Neumann Residence which houses college-age men preparing for the priesthood.

Among many moving encounters between the faithful and Pope Benedict, a special one occurred in the intimacy of the chapel at St. Joseph's Seminary. There, the Holy Father greeted young people with disabilities and their families. He moved slowly among them extending his hands in blessing and offering words of greeting and encouragement. The Archdiocesan Deaf Choir and the Cathedral of St. Patrick's Young Singers added spirit to the Pope's visit with beautiful signing and singing.

In his remarks, Pope Benedict emphasized the importance of every person's contribution. Surrounded by the beauty of human life, the Pontiff was clear: everyone has something to contribute. His Holiness also reminded the gathering that it is the suffering of Christ which transforms:

The pontiff is welcomed to St. Joseph's ■■■
Seminary by clergy members
and Cardinal Egan, seen at right.
© BOB REERS/CATHOLIC NEW YORK

The Pope, arms extended, waves greeting upon arrival ■■■
at the seminary. Cardinal Edward Egan of New York
and others in background.
© BOB REERS/CATHOLIC NEW YORK

Through his Cross, Jesus in fact draws us into his saving love (cf. Jn 12:32) and in so doing shows us the way ahead - the way of hope which transfigures us all, so that we too, become bearers of that hope and charity for others.

The Holy Father then emphasized the power of their prayers. Alluding to his recent birthday and the passing of years, he asked those present to pray for the world and for him as he does for them.

Following the meeting, Pope Benedict made an unscheduled visit to the sick bed of the noted theologian, Cardinal Avery Dulles, SJ.

■■■ Pope Benedict XVI offers a friendly smile for the camera.
© MARY DIBIASE BLAICH, CATHOLIC NEW YORK

The Pope greets Msgr. Kevin Sullivan, ■■■ Executive Director of New York Catholic Charities.
© MARY DIBIASE BLAICH, CATHOLIC NEW YORK

■■■ Boy kissing pope's ring.
© MARY DIBIASE BLAICH, CATHOLIC NEW YORK

■■■ The Pope gently touches head of boy.
© MARY DIBIASE BLAICH, CATHOLIC NEW YORK

■■■ The Holy Father with girls who presented him with a gift.
© MARY DIBIASE BLAICH, CATHOLIC NEW YORK

■■■ Mother (Christine Donohue) with daughter
(Mary Christine Donohue).
© MARY DIBIASE BLAICH, CATHOLIC NEW YORK

■■■ The members of New York Archdiocesan Deaf Choir sing.
© MARY DIBIASE BLAICH, CATHOLIC NEW YORK

■■■ Bishop Nicholas DiMarzio of Brooklyn blesses a child.
© MARY DIBIASE BLAICH, CATHOLIC NEW YORK

- Rally with Seminarians and Young People at St. Joseph's Seminary -

Yonkers, NY
Saturday, April 19th
5:15 p.m.

After visiting Cardinal Dulles, Pope Benedict proceeded to the Seminary's backfields, where a large crowd of 25,000 young people had been waiting since noon. In preparation for the encounter with the Holy Father, the Archdiocese sponsored a youth rally with music, prayers, and entertainment. Anticipation, which had been growing all day, reached a fever pitch as the Popemobile came into view. Upon seeing the Holy Father, deafening cheers and thunderous applause erupted from the crowd.

■■■ Girls from Immaculate Conception School, the Bronx, hold banner.
© CHRIS SHERIDAN CATHOLIC NEW YORK

When he reached the large stage, already filled with cardinals and bishops, the young people welcomed the Holy Father with more chants and cheers. Energy pervaded the gathering, and the Pope was visibly elated by the dynamism of the event. Responding to the call of the crowd, he left his chair to greet those closest to him.

Able to quiet the crowd for a brief moment, Cardinal Egan welcomed the Pope with warm words of affection. Noting the many voices that compete for the hearts and minds of young people, His Eminence thanked the Holy Father for coming and offering *"another voice—the voice of the Vicar of Christ, inviting and urging them to justice, compassion, honor, cleanness of heart, and a habit of prayer."*

Shot of the large crowd on hand. ■■■
© CHRIS SHERIDAN, CATHOLIC NEW YORK

Homemade sign says a lot, "The Pope Brings Hope." ■■■
© CHRIS SHERIDAN, CATHOLIC NEW YORK

Three representatives then greeted the Pope on behalf of the diverse gathering. Following a Slavic custom of greeting guests with bread, loaves from around the world were presented to the Holy Father, symbolizing the cultural backgrounds and traditions of all present. Next, the seminarians and young people sang "Happy Birthday" to the Pontiff in German and gave him a spiritual bouquet and a book on the history of the Church in New York. The Holy Father also received images of six individuals who were born in or served in New York and have been recognized for their lives of heroic virtue: St. Elizabeth Ann Seton, St. Frances Xavier Cabrini, St. John Neumann, Blessed Kateri Tekakwitha, Venerable Pierre Toussaint, and Padre Felix Varela. After the presentation of gifts, a small band led the participants in songs to mark the anniversary of Pope Benedict's election as the Successor of Peter.

The Holy Father then addressed the gathering. During his talk, the beautiful and moving interaction between the Pope and his young flock continued as his words were met with joyful outbursts. At one point, the group's chant "We love you!" was received with a genuine and humble "Thank you!" from the Pope.

In his address, His Holiness shared with the audience *"some thoughts about being disciples of Jesus Christ."* To this end, he mentioned the six images given to him earlier of *"ordinary men and women who grew up to lead extraordinary lives."* He noted that *"any one of us could be among them, for there is no stereotype to this group, no single mold."* Speaking of these heroic lives of faith that witnessed Christ to others in years gone by, the Pope asked the simple question: *"And what of today?"*

■■■ Three young seminarians in front row.
© CHRIS SHERIDAN, CATHOLIC NEW YORK

■■■ The massive crowd reacts with excitement during the rally.
© CHRIS SHERIDAN, CATHOLIC NEW YORK

All eyes were on the stage when ■■■
Pope Benedict XVI arrived for rally with
young people at St. Joseph's Seminary
© CHRIS SHERIDAN, CATHOLIC NEW YORK

■■■ Young women pray during Pope Benedict XVI's
rally with youths at St. Joseph's Seminary.
© CHRIS SHERIDAN, CATHOLIC NEW YORK

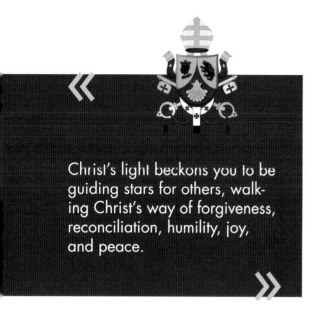

Christ's light beckons you to be guiding stars for others, walking Christ's way of forgiveness, reconciliation, humility, joy, and peace.

The Pontiff spoke about the difficulty of giving such a witness in today's society in which so many hardships threaten to stifle hope and add to our confusion. He movingly related his own experience as a teenager living under the *"sinister regime"* of Nazism which he described as a *"monster."* While recognizing the many opportunities afforded the youth of the United States to develop in an environment that nurtures the good, the beautiful, and the true, the Pope reminded the gathering that dark and destructive forces remain. To counter such darkness, Pope Benedict proposed the beauty of truth:

Dear friends, truth is not an imposition. Nor is it simply a set of rules. It is a discovery of the One who never fails us; the One whom we can always trust…ultimately truth is a person: Jesus Christ.

The Pope again encouraged the young people and seminarians to fix their *"gaze on our saints"* as a means to discover Christ. As the saints' lives radiated the light of Christ, the Holy Father reminded each person that: *"Christ's light beckons you to be guiding stars for others, walking Christ's way of forgiveness, reconciliation, humility, joy, and peace."*

■■■ The Pope reaches out to the young people at the rally as Cardinal Egan smiles in the background.
© CHRIS SHERIDAN, CATHOLIC NEW YORK

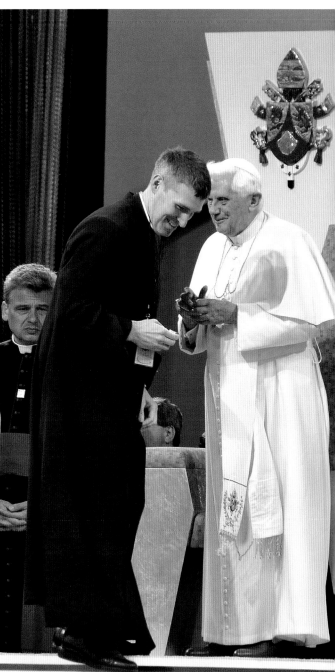

■■■ The Pope shakes hands with Thomas Zwilling.
© CHRIS SHERIDAN, CATHOLIC NEW YORK

■■■ Pope Benedict XVI greets seminarian
on stage at the rally.
© CHRIS SHERIDAN, CATHOLIC NEW YORK

■■■ The crowd of young people let their enthusiasm
show at many points throughout the rally.
© CHRIS SHERIDAN, CATHOLIC NEW YORK

The Pope next spoke about *"four essential aspects of the trea-sure of our faith: personal prayer and silence, liturgical prayer, charity in action, and vocations."* His Holiness stressed the impor-tance of developing a life of prayer to build and sustain a per-sonal relationship with God. Reminding those present of the need for silent contemplation, he asked the gathering: *"Do you leave space to hear God's whisper, calling you forth into goodness?"* Pope Benedict then spoke of the importance of participating in the grandeur of the Church's sacraments which draw the faithful into an encounter with the saving work of Christ. After speaking of the need to serve others the Pope, to the cheers of the crowd, shared a word about vocations. He began by highlighting mar-riage and family life which foster all vocations. Next, he urged the seminarians present to *"deepen your friendship with Jesus the Good Shepherd"* and to *"talk heart to heart with him"* in order to be holy priests. Finally, the Pontiff reminded the gathering of the importance of the charisms that consecrated men and women live in prophetic witness to the Gospel and urged young people to inquire about them.

At the end of his remarks, the Pope told the young people once again that *"the hope which never disappoints is Jesus Christ"* and noted that His selfless way is made known to us by the saints and nourished by the Church. He urged the gathering to follow the examples of the saints and be friends of Jesus:

■■■ The pontiff and Cardinal Egan
share a happy moment on stage.
© CHRIS SHERIDAN, CATHOLIC NEW YORK

You are Christ's disciples today. Shine his light upon this great city and beyond. Show the world the reason for the hope that resonates within you. Tell others about the truth that sets you free.

After finishing his remarks, the Holy Father rose to the applause of the crowd. However, after a word from his secretary, His Holiness sat down and humbly admitted, *"I forgot my Spanish part."* The crowd again erupted with cheers, eager to hear his message to the Hispanic community.

The gathering then sang a litany of the saints before praying the Lord's Prayer. Next, Cardinal Egan presented fifteen young people to the Holy Father. The Pope then blessed the gathering and passed through the crowd in the Popemobile before returning to Manhattan for the evening.

April | 20

– "Ground Zero" –
New York City
Sunday, April 20th
9:30 a.m.

By the evening of September 11, 2001, they were already calling the site "Ground Zero." The term refers to the point where an explosion occurs. These two words captured the physical and emotional trauma of a day that took nearly 3,000 lives and forever changed millions more.

The Twin Towers were the most famous and visible components of the World Trade Center, a seven building, sixteen-acre site in lower Manhattan. More than 150,000 people arrived to work or visit at the Trade Center each day. As the tallest structures in New York City, the sight of the Twin Towers was familiar to people around the world, and the people of the world came to the Towers. Indeed, more than eighty nationalities have been recorded among the victims of the attack.

Tuesday, September 11th was a beautiful late summer day in New York. Tens of thousands of people were beginning their workday when, at 8:46 a.m., a passenger plane hijacked by terrorists crashed into the North Tower. A second hijacked airliner crashed into the South Tower sixteen minutes later. By 10:30 that morning, both Towers had collapsed. That same morning, a third hijacked airliner crashed into the Pentagon in Washington, DC. As passengers attempted to retake control of a fourth hijacked plane, it crashed in Shanksville, Pennsylvania without reaching its intended target in the nation's capital. New Yorkers, Americans, and people throughout the world struggled to comprehend the enormity and the cruelty of the attacks.

Since 2001, "Ground Zero" has gone from a rescue site to a clean-up site to a construction site. However, in all these incarnations, it remains for many people a site of deep significance. The searing losses of that day continuously draw people to reflect, to remember, and to pray. As one among hundreds of thousands of pilgrims over these past seven years, this Pilgrim Pontiff made a uniquely powerful visit of prayer, hope, and consolation.

Away from the festive atmosphere of cheering crowds, the principal cellist of the New York Philharmonic expressed the emotions of those gathered for the Pope's visit with the somber music of a Bach suite. With New York City Mayor Michael Bloomberg, New York Governor David Paterson, New Jersey Governor John Corzine and other city and state officials looking on, the Holy Father arrived at "Ground Zero." After descending the flag-lined ramp in his Popemobile, Pope Benedict walked the last fifty yards with Cardinal Egan. Coming to the reflecting pool, he immediately knelt in silent prayer. Rising, he stepped forward to light a large white candle. Then, His Holiness prayed aloud for the lost, the grieving, and for peace in the world, concluding his prayer by invoking divine wisdom and compassion:

God of understanding,
overwhelmed by the magnitude of this tragedy,
we seek your light and guidance
as we confront such terrible events.
Grant that those whose lives were spared
may live so that the lives lost here
may not have been lost in vain.
Comfort and console us,
strengthen us in hope,
and give us the wisdom and courage
to work tirelessly for a world
where true peace and love reign
among nations and in the hearts of all.

Following the prayer, Pope Benedict blessed the ground with holy water and took time to greet family members of the lost and representatives of the heroic emergency services who were among the first responders on 9/11. After these personal greetings, the Holy Father departed the site in the Popemobile. Pope Benedict arrived at Ground Zero; he left Holy Ground.

© CHRIS SHERIDAN, CATHOLIC NEW YORK

© CHRIS SHERIDAN, CATHOLIC NEW YORK

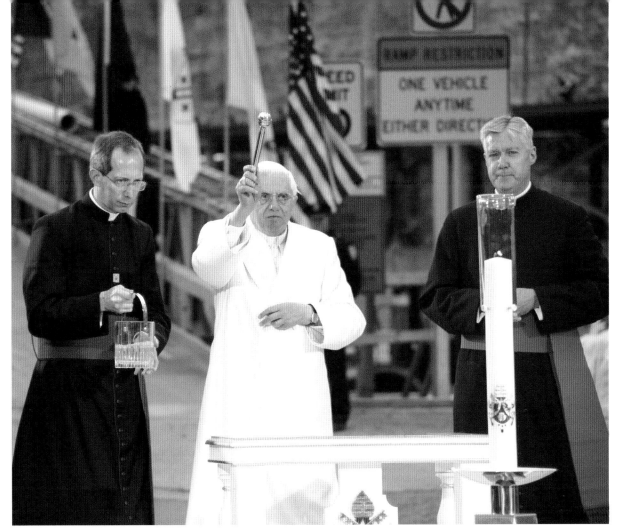

- Celebration of Holy Mass at Yankee Stadium -

The Bronx, NY
Sunday, April 20th
2:30 p.m.

Following lunch at the residence of Archbishop Migliore, the Holy Father traveled to Yankee Stadium for the third and final papal Mass in this historic ballpark, which will be razed at the end of the 2008 season. The Mass was preceded by a two-hour "Concert of Hope," which included performances by the West Point Cadets, Dana, the Harlem Gospel Choir, Ronan Tynan, José Feliciano, and Harry Connick Jr. Entering the warning-track of the stadium in the outfield, His Holiness greeted the 57,000 worshippers from his Popemobile.

In his welcoming remarks, Cardinal Egan outlined the unique nature of the gathering which represented all 195 archdioceses, dioceses and eparchies in the United States. In the beginning of his homily, the Holy Father acknowledged the significance of this representation:

People start entering the Yankee Stadium. ■■■
© PATRICK DANCZEWSKI

The presence around this altar of the Successor of Peter, his brother bishops and priests, and deacons, men and women religious, and lay faithful from throughout the fifty states of the Union, eloquently manifests our communion in the Catholic faith which comes to us from the Apostles.

He also spoke of the five archdioceses that had special cause to celebrate as 2008 marked the bicentennial of their establishment: Baltimore, New York, Boston, Philadelphia, and Bardstown (now Louisville).

The Pontiff returned once again to the theme of the unity of the Church based on *"the Word of God made flesh in Jesus Christ Our Lord,"* and stressed the importance of transcending

■■■ Harry Connick Jr. was one of the headline performers who entertained the crowd before the Papal Mass began.
© MARY DIBIASE BLAICH, CATHOLIC NEW YORK

Famed tenor Marcello Giordani ■■■
hits a high note.
© MARY DIBIASE BLAICH, CATHOLIC NEW YORK

■■■ Jose Feliciano strums his guitar to the crowd's delight.
© MARY DIBIASE BLAICH, CATHOLIC NEW YORK

Gospel choir sings behind Stephanie Mills. ■■■
© MARY DIBIASE BLAICH, CATHOLIC NEW YORK

■■■ Heavenly dancers kept their props soaring before the Mass.
© MARY DIBIASE-BLAICH, CATHOLIC NEW YORK

Pre-Mass entertainment featured ■■■
a grand "flying" spectacular.
© ÉDITIONS DU SIGNE

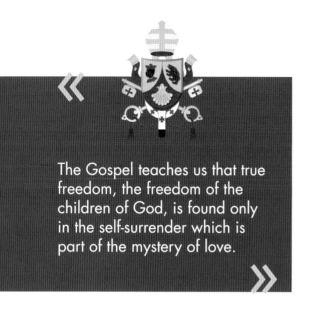

The Gospel teaches us that true freedom, the freedom of the children of God, is found only in the self-surrender which is part of the mystery of love.

the divisions that arise from *"human limitations and weakness."* He linked ecclesial unity to authority and obedience, concepts that represent *"a stumbling stone"* in contemporary society with its quest for personal freedom. In contrast to such an understanding, the Holy Father conveyed how: *"The Gospel teaches us that true freedom, the freedom of the children of God, is found only in the self-surrender which is part of the mystery of love."* Such authentic freedom is also characterized by the *"conversion to truth"* and acting in accord with God's will. For the Pope, freedom without truth and goodness is not freedom at all.

Real doves fly across the field after their release prior to the Papal Mass. ■■■

■■■ The Popemobile delivers its important passengers.
© EILEEN MILLER, CATHOLIC NEW YORK

This sign makes a request ■■■
of the Holy Father.
© MARIA R. BASTONE, CATHOLIC NEW YORK

The crowd waves their yellow and white bandanas in reacting to the ■■■
appearance of the Popemobile on the field at Yankee Stadium.
© MARIA R. BASTONE, CATHOLIC NEW YORK

■■■ Congregation waits for the Pope's arrival.

■■■ Profile of four nuns during Mass.

Another woman praying during Papal Mass. ■■■

■■■ Overall view of the altar platform at Papal Mass in Yankee Stadium.

■■■ Pope Benedict XVI waves to the congregation at the Papal Mass at Yankee Stadium.
© MARIA R. BASTONE, CATHOLIC NEW YORK

Close-up of Pope Benedict XVI ■■■
during the Mass at Yankee Stadium.
© MARIA R. BASTONE, CATHOLIC NEW YORK

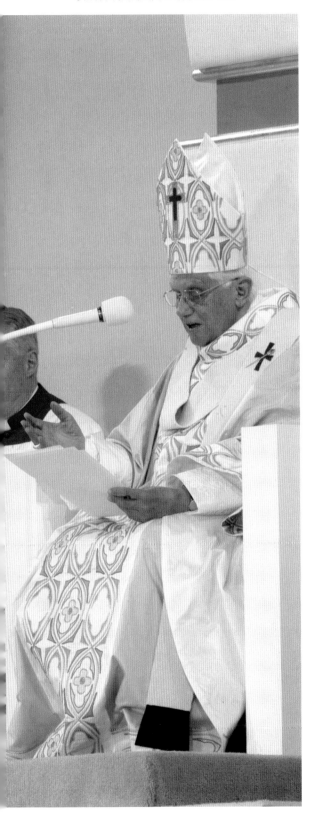

Pope Benedict commented too on the importance of religious freedom. He noted the benefits such freedom has brought to Catholics in the United States, including the ability to participate in civic life and bring *"their deepest moral convictions to the public square."* With this in mind, His Holiness spoke of the continuing challenge to Catholics in America:

Today's celebration is more than an occasion of gratitude for graces received. It is also a summons to move forward with firm resolve to use wisely the blessings of freedom, in order to build a future of hope for coming generations.

He also summoned Catholics, and all Christians in the United States, to allow the petition from the Lord's Prayer, *"Thy kingdom come,"* to shape their *"minds and hearts."* In a particularly powerful set of remarks, the Pope described the task of praying and living this petition:

It means facing the challenges of present and future with confidence in Christ's victory and a commitment to extending his reign. It means not losing heart in the face of resistance, adversity and scandal. It means overcoming every separation between faith and life, and countering false gospels of freedom and happiness. It also means rejecting a false dichotomy between faith and political life... It means working to enrich American society and culture with the beauty and truth of the Gospel, and never losing sight of that great hope which gives meaning and value to all the other hopes which inspire our lives.

He added a direct personal challenge to his listeners:

And this, dear friends, is the particular challenge which the Successor of Saint Peter sets before you today. As 'a chosen people, a royal priesthood, a holy nation,' follow faithfully in the footsteps of those who have gone before you! Hasten the coming of God's Kingdom in this land! Past generations have left you an impressive legacy. In our day too, the Catholic community in this nation has been outstanding in its prophetic witness in the defense of life, in the education of the young, in care for the poor, the sick and the stranger in your midst. On these solid foundations, the future of the Church in America must even now begin to rise!

the future of the Church in America must even now begin to rise!

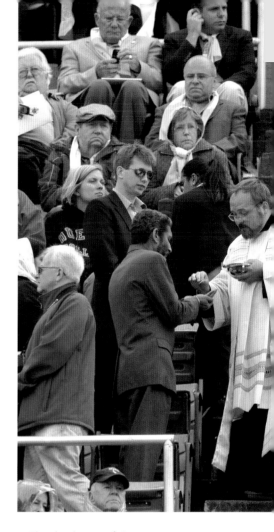

The distribution of Communion saw ■■■
priests stationed in all corners
of Yankee Stadium.
© MARIA R. BASTONE, CATHOLIC NEW YORK

■■■ A priest giving Communion to a woman.
© EILEEN MILLER, CATHOLIC NEW YORK

■■■ Bishop William Murphy, the Bishop of Rockville Centre, stands among dozens of prelates.
© MARIA R. BASTONE, CATHOLIC NEW YORK

Next, Pope Benedict again directed his attention to the young, asking them to *"step forward and take up the responsibility which your faith in Christ sets before you!"* In his final remarks, he was interrupted by applause as he called upon young people to defend *"the most defenseless of all human beings, the unborn child in the mother's womb."* Applause erupted a second time a few moments later when he asked the young to open their hearts to *"the Lord's call to follow him in the priesthood and the religious life."*

Following the final blessing, the Holy Father remained at his chair with arms outstretched, acknowledging the deafening applause of the crowd. Then, to the music of Beethoven's "Ode to Joy," the Pope left the sanctuary. As the recessional made its way across the wonderfully colored infield, the Pope shook the hands of bishops, priests, and members of the laity. Before entering the Yankee clubhouse, which had been converted into a temporary sacristy, His Holiness paused several times to bless the faithful.

After a few minutes, Pope Benedict emerged from the dugout with this personal secretary, Msgr. Georg Ganswein. Accompanied by Cardinal Egan, they entered the Popemobile which slowly brought the Successor of Peter around the perimeter of the outfield. Having transferred to a limousine, the papal entourage then returned to the Permanent Mission of the Holy See to United Nations to prepare for the departure from the United States.

As they did to commemorate the Masses celebrated at the stadium by Popes Paul VI and John Paul II, the Knights of Columbus commissioned a bronze plaque to be placed in Yankee Stadium's Monument Park to mark the Mass celebrated by Pope Benedict XVI. Prior to the Mass, His Holiness blessed the plaque in a private ceremony.

Papal Visits to Yankee Stadium

The famous "house that Ruth built" at East 161st Street and River Avenue in the South Bronx has been home to Major League Baseball's New York Yankees since 1923. The legendary diamond hosted two previous papal Masses. Pope Paul VI celebrated Mass at the Stadium during his one day journey to the United Nations and New York on October 4, 1965. A crowd of over 80,000 people was present on that Feast of St. Francis of Assisi to hear the Pontiff preach on the importance of loving and serving a peace founded on moral and religious principles. Fourteen years later, John Paul II celebrated with a similar number of worshippers. The Holy Father spoke of the Christian call to love and serve the poor as brothers and sisters in Christ.

- Departure from
John F. Kennedy International Airport -

Queens, NY
Sunday, April 20th
8:00 p.m.

Let us turn to Jesus! He alone is the way that leads to eternal happiness, the truth who satisfies the deepest longings of every heart, and the life who brings ever new joy and hope, to us and to our world. Amen.

- From the closing words of Pope's Benedict's homily at Yankee Stadium

More than 4,000 of the faithful crowded into Hangar 19 at John F. Kennedy Airport in the Diocese of Brooklyn to bid farewell to Pope Benedict. For two hours prior to his arrival, the multi-ethnic and enthusiastic crowd enjoyed a program of music and prayed the Glorious Mysteries of the Rosary in the many languages of the diocese.

The Holy Father arrived with Vice President and Mrs. Dick Cheney. Following the United States and Vatican anthems, Vice President Cheney thanked His Holiness for his visit to the United States and spoke of the countless ways in which he has become a source of inspiration for so many:

Your Holiness, nearly 57 years have passed since the day of your ordination as a priest in June 1951. You might have found it hard to imagine then that you would stand before all humanity as a teacher, a statesman, and the shepherd of more than a billion souls. That is what God has called you to do.

In these 57 years, your wisdom and your pastoral gifts have been extraordinary blessings to our world. In these six days, you've shared those blessings very directly for the people of the United States. Your presence has honored our country. Although you must leave us now, your words and the memory of this week will stay with us. For that, we are truly and humbly grateful.

■■■ Pope Benedict XVI gives a farewell address to a crowd gathered in a hanger at JFK International Airport in New York April 20, 2008.
© CNS PHOTO/NANCY WIECHEC

Pope Benedict then offered his own words of gratitude to the many people who assisted in making his Apostolic Journey possible. He spoke also of the memorable experiences of his visit and the hospitality extended to him at every turn.

After the Pope's remarks, Bishop Nicholas DiMarzio of Brooklyn led several school children of the diocese to the Holy Father who presented him with flowers. Pope Benedict left for his plane to the applause of thousands and with the best wishes of a grateful Church, city, and nation.

Bishop Nicholas DiMarzio of Brooklyn, ■■■
looks on as Eric Floes, 12,
presents a bouquet of flowers to
Pope Benedict XVI during a departure
ceremony at JFK International Airport
in New York April 20.
© CNS PHOTO/NANCY WIECHEC

Texts of all addresses, homilies, and official statements

WELCOMING CEREMONY

ADDRESS OF HIS HOLINESS BENEDICT XVI

South Lawn of the White House, Washington, DC.
Wednesday, April 16, 2008

Mr. President,

Thank you for your gracious words of welcome on behalf of the people of the United States of America. I deeply appreciate your invitation to visit this great country. My visit coincides with an important moment in the life of the Catholic community in America: the celebration of the two-hundredth anniversary of the elevation of the country's first Diocese – Baltimore – to a metropolitan Archdiocese, and the establishment of the Sees of New York, Boston, Philadelphia and Louisville. Yet I am happy to be here as a guest of all Americans. I come as a friend, a preacher of the Gospel and one with great respect for this vast pluralistic society. America's Catholics have made, and continue to make, an excellent contribution to the life of their country. As I begin my visit, I trust that my presence will be a source of renewal and hope for the Church in the United States, and strengthen the resolve of Catholics to contribute ever more responsibly to the life of this nation, of which they are proud to be citizens.

From the dawn of the Republic, America's quest for freedom has been guided by the conviction that the principles governing political and social life are intimately linked to a moral order based on the dominion of God the Creator. The framers of this nation's founding documents drew upon this conviction when they proclaimed the "self-evident truth" that all men are created equal and endowed with inalienable rights grounded in the laws of nature and of nature's God. The course of American history demonstrates the difficulties, the struggles, and the great intellectual and moral resolve which were demanded to shape a society which faithfully embodied these noble principles. In that process, which forged the soul of the nation, religious beliefs were a constant inspiration and driving force, as for example in the struggle against slavery and in the civil rights movement. In our time too, particularly in moments of crisis, Americans continue to find their strength in a commitment to this patrimony of shared ideals and aspirations.

In the next few days, I look forward to meeting not only with America's Catholic community, but with other Christian communities and representatives of the many religious traditions present in this country. Historically, not only Catholics, but all believers have found here the freedom to worship God in accordance with the dictates of their conscience, while at the same time being accepted as part of a commonwealth in which each individual and group can make its voice heard. As the nation faces the increasingly complex political and ethical issues of our time, I am confident that the American people will find in their religious beliefs a precious source of insight and an inspiration to pursue reasoned, responsible and respectful dialogue in the effort to build a more humane and free society.

Freedom is not only a gift, but also a summons to personal responsibility. Americans know this from experience – almost every town in this country has its monuments honoring those who sacrificed their lives in defense of freedom, both at home and abroad. The preservation of freedom calls for the cultivation of virtue, self-discipline, sacrifice for the common good and a sense of responsibility towards the less fortunate. It also demands the courage to engage in civic life and to bring one's deepest beliefs and values to reasoned public debate. In a word, freedom is ever new. It is a challenge held out to each generation, and it must constantly be won over for the cause of good (cf. *Spe Salvi*, 24). Few have understood this as clearly as the late Pope John Paul II. In reflecting on the spiritual victory of freedom over totalitarianism in his native Poland and in eastern Europe, he reminded us that history shows, time and again, that "in a world without truth, freedom loses its foundation," and a democracy without values can lose its very soul (cf. *Centesimus Annus*, 46). Those prophetic words in some sense echo the conviction of President Washington, expressed in his Farewell Address, that religion and morality represent "indispensable supports" of political prosperity.

The Church, for her part, wishes to contribute to building a world ever more worthy of the human person, created in the image and likeness of God (cf. Gen 1:26-27). She is convinced that faith sheds new light on all things, and that the Gospel reveals the noble vocation and sublime destiny of every man and woman (cf. *Gaudium et Spes*, 10). Faith also gives us the strength to respond to our high calling and the hope that inspires us to work for an ever more just and fraternal society. Democracy can only flourish, as your founding fathers realized, when political leaders and those whom they represent are guided by truth and bring the wisdom born of firm moral principle to decisions affecting the life and future of the nation.

For well over a century, the United States of America has played an important role in the international community. On Friday, God willing, I will have the honor of addressing the United Nations Organization, where I hope to encourage the efforts under way to make that institution an ever more effective voice for the legitimate aspirations of all the world's peoples. On this, the sixtieth anniversary of the Universal Declaration of Human Rights, the need for global solidarity is as urgent as ever, if all people are to live in a way worthy of their dignity – as brothers and sisters dwelling in the same house and around that table which God's bounty has set for all his children. America has traditionally shown herself generous in meeting immediate human needs, fostering development and offering relief to the victims of natural catastrophes. I am confident that this concern for the greater human family will continue to find expression in support for the patient efforts of international diplomacy to resolve conflicts and promote progress. In this way, coming generations will be able to live in a world where truth, freedom and justice can flourish – a world where the God-given dignity and rights of every man, woman and child are cherished, protected and effectively advanced.

Mr. President, dear friends: as I begin my visit to the United States, I express once more my gratitude for your invitation, my joy to be in your midst, and my fervent prayers that Almighty God will confirm this nation and its people in the ways of justice, prosperity and peace. God bless America!

FINAL HOLY SEE - US JOINT STATEMENT

Oval Office of the White House
Wednesday, April 16, 2008

At the end of the private meeting between the Holy Father Benedict XVI and U.S. President George W. Bush, the Holy See and the Office of the President of the United States of America released a joint declaration:

President Bush, on behalf of all Americans, welcomed the Holy Father, wished him a happy birthday, and thanked him for the spiritual and moral guidance which he offers to the whole human family. The President wished the Pope every success in his Apostolic Journey and in his address at the United Nations, and expressed appreciation for the Pope's upcoming visit to "Ground Zero" in New York.

During their meeting, the Holy Father and the President discussed a number of topics of common interest to the Holy See and the United States of America, including moral and religious considerations to which both parties are committed: the respect of the dignity of the human person; the defense and promotion of life, matrimony and the family; the education of future generations; human rights and religious freedom; sustainable development and the struggle against poverty and pandemics, especially in Africa. In regard to the latter, the Holy Father welcomed the United States' substantial financial contributions in this area. The two reaffirmed their total rejection of terrorism as well as the manipulation of religion to justify immoral and violent acts against innocents. They further touched on the need to confront terrorism with appropriate means that respect the human person and his or her rights.

The Holy Father and the President devoted considerable time in their discussions to the Middle East, in particular resolving the Israel-Palestinian conflict in line with the vision of two states living side-by-side in peace and security, their mutual support for the sovereignty and independence of Lebanon, and their common concern for the situation in Iraq and particularly the precarious state of Christian communities there and elsewhere in the region. The Holy Father and the President expressed hope for an end to violence and for a prompt and comprehensive solution to the crises which afflict the region.

The Holy Father and the President also considered the situation in Latin America with reference, among other matters, to immigrants, and the need for a coordinated policy regarding immigration, especially their humane treatment and the well being of their families.

CELEBRATION OF VESPERS AND MEETING WITH THE BISHOPS OF THE UNITED STATES OF AMERICA

ADDRESS OF HIS HOLINESS BENEDICT XVI

National Shrine of the Immaculate Conception in Washington, DC.
Wednesday, April 16, 2008

Dear Brother Bishops,

It gives me great joy to greet you today, at the start of my visit to this country, and I thank Cardinal George for the gracious words he has addressed to me on your behalf. I want to thank all of you, especially the Officers of the Episcopal Conference, for the hard work that has gone into the preparation of this visit. My grateful appreciation goes also to the staff and volunteers of the National Shrine, who have welcomed us here this evening. American Catholics are noted for their loyal devotion to the see of Peter. My pastoral visit here is an opportunity to strengthen further the bonds of communion that unite us. We began by celebrating Evening Prayer in this Basilica dedicated to the Immaculate Conception of the Blessed Virgin Mary, a shrine of special significance to American Catholics, right in the heart of your capital city. Gathered in prayer with Mary, Mother of Jesus, we lovingly commend to our heavenly Father the people of God in every part of the United States.

For the Catholic communities of Boston, New York, Philadelphia and Louisville, this is a year of particular celebration, as it marks the bicentenary of the establishment of these local Churches as dioceses. I join you in giving thanks for the many graces granted to the Church there during these two centuries. As this year also marks the bicentenary of the elevation of the founding see of Baltimore to an archdiocese, it gives me an opportunity to recall with admiration and gratitude the life and ministry of John Carroll, the first Bishop of Baltimore – a worthy leader of the Catholic community in your newly independent nation. His tireless efforts to spread the Gospel in the vast territory under his care laid the foundations for the ecclesial life of your country and enabled the Church in America to grow to maturity. Today the Catholic community you serve is one of the largest in the world, and one of the most influential. How important it is, then, to let your light so shine before your fellow citizens and before the world, "that they may see your good works and give glory to your Father who is in heaven" (Mt 5:16).

Many of the people to whom John Carroll and his fellow bishops were ministering two centuries ago had travelled from distant lands. The diversity of their origins is reflected in the rich variety of ecclesial life in present-day America. Brother Bishops, I want to encourage you and your communities to continue to welcome the immigrants who join your ranks today, to share their joys and hopes, to support them in their sorrows and trials, and to help them flourish in their new home. This, indeed, is what your fellow countrymen have done for generations. From the beginning, they have opened their doors to the tired, the poor, the "huddled masses yearning to breathe free" (cf. sonnet inscribed on the Statue of Liberty). These are the people whom America has made her own.

Of those who came to build a new life here, many were able to make good use of the resources and opportunities that they found, and to attain a high level of prosperity. Indeed, the people of this country are known for their great vitality and creativity. They are also known for their generosity. After the attack on the Twin Towers in September 2001, and again after Hurricane Katrina in 2005, Americans displayed their readiness to come to the aid of their brothers and sisters in need. On the international level, the contribution made by the people of America to relief and rescue operations after the tsunami of December 2004 is a further illustration of this compassion. Let me express my particular appreciation for the many forms of humanitarian assistance provided by American Catholics through Catholic Charities and other agencies. Their generosity has borne fruit in the care shown to the poor and needy, and in the energy that has gone into building the nationwide network of Catholic parishes, hospitals, schools and universities. All of this gives great cause for thanksgiving.

America is also a land of great faith. Your people are remarkable for their religious fervor and they take pride in belonging to a worshipping community. They have confidence in God, and they do not hesitate to bring moral arguments rooted in biblical faith into their public discourse. Respect for freedom of religion is deeply ingrained in the American consciousness – a fact which has contributed to this country's attraction for generations of immigrants, seeking a home where they can worship freely in accordance with their beliefs.

In this connection, I happily acknowledge the presence among you of bishops from all the venerable Eastern Churches in communion with the Successor of Peter, whom I greet with special joy. Dear Brothers, I ask you to assure your communities of my deep affection and my continued prayers, both for them and for the many brothers and sisters who remain in their land of origin. Your presence here is a reminder of the courageous witness to Christ of so many members of your communities, often amid suffering, in their respective homelands. It is also a great enrichment of the ecclesial life of America, giving vivid expression to the Church's catholicity and the variety of her liturgical and spiritual traditions.

It is in this fertile soil, nourished from so many different sources, that all of you, Brother Bishops, are called to sow the seeds of the Gospel today. This leads me to ask how, in the twenty-first century, a bishop can best fulfill the call to "make all things new in Christ, our hope"? How can he lead his people to "an encounter with the living God," the source of that life-transforming hope of which the Gospel speaks (cf. Spe Salvi, 4)? Perhaps he needs to begin by clearing away some of the barriers to such an encounter. While it is true that this country is marked by a genuinely religious spirit, the subtle influence of secularism can nevertheless color the way people allow their faith to influence their behavior. Is it consistent to profess our beliefs in church on Sunday, and then during the week to promote business practices or medical procedures contrary to those beliefs? Is it consistent for practicing Catholics to ignore or exploit the poor and the marginalized, to promote sexual behavior contrary to Catholic moral teaching, or to adopt positions that contradict the right to life of every human being from conception to natural death? Any tendency to treat religion as a private matter must be resisted. Only when their faith permeates every aspect of their lives do Christians become truly open to the transforming power of the Gospel.

For an affluent society, a further obstacle to an encounter with the living God lies in the subtle influence of materialism, which can all too easily focus the attention on the hundredfold, which God promises now in this time, at the expense of the eternal life which he promises in the age to come (cf. Mk 10:30). People today need to be reminded of the ultimate purpose of their lives. They need to recognize that implanted within them is a deep thirst for God. They need to be given opportunities to drink from the wells of his infinite love. It is easy to be entranced by the almost unlimited possibilities that science and technology place before us; it is easy to make the mistake of thinking we can obtain by our own efforts the fulfillment of our deepest needs. This is an illusion. Without God, who alone bestows upon us what we by ourselves cannot attain (cf. Spe Salvi, 31), our lives are ultimately empty. People need to be constantly reminded to cultivate a relationship with him who came that we might have life in abundance (cf. Jn 10:10). The goal of all our pastoral and catechetical work, the object of our preaching, and the focus of our sacramental ministry should be to help people establish and nurture that living relationship with "Christ Jesus, our hope" (1 Tim 1:1).

In a society which values personal freedom and autonomy, it is easy to lose sight of our dependence on others as well as the responsibilities that we bear towards them. This emphasis on individualism has even affected the Church (cf. Spe Salvi, 13-15), giving rise to a form of piety which sometimes emphasizes our private relationship with God at the expense of our calling to be members of a redeemed community. Yet from the beginning, God saw that "it is not good for man to be alone" (Gen 2:18). We were created as social beings who find fulfillment only in love – for God and for our neighbor. If we are truly to gaze upon him who is the source of our joy, we need to do so as members of the people of God (cf. Spe Salvi, 14). If this seems countercultural, that is simply further evidence of the urgent need for a renewed evangelization of culture.

Here in America, you are blessed with a Catholic laity of considerable cultural diversity, who place their wide-ranging gifts at the service of the Church and of society at large. They look to you to offer them encouragement, leadership and direction. In an age that is saturated with information, the importance of providing sound formation in the faith cannot be overstated. American Catholics have traditionally placed a high value on religious education, both in schools and in the context of adult formation programs. These need to be maintained and expanded. The many generous men and women who devote themselves to charitable activity need to be helped to renew their dedication through a "formation of the heart": an "encounter with God in Christ which awakens their love and opens their spirits to others" (Deus Caritas Est, 31). At a time when advances in medical science bring new hope to many, they also give rise to previously unimagined ethical challenges. This makes it more important than ever to offer thorough formation in the Church's moral teaching to Catholics engaged in health care. Wise guidance is needed in all these apostolates, so that they may bear abundant fruit; if they are truly to promote the integral good of the human person, they too need to be made new in Christ our hope.

As preachers of the Gospel and leaders of the Catholic community, you are also called to participate in the exchange of ideas in the public square, helping to shape cultural attitudes. In a context where free speech is valued, and where vigorous and honest debate is encouraged, yours is a respected voice that has much to offer to the discussion of the pressing social and moral questions of the day. By ensuring that the Gospel is clearly heard, you not only form the people of your own community, but in view of the global reach of mass communication, you help to spread the message of Christian hope throughout the world.

Clearly, the Church's influence on public debate takes place on many different levels. In the United States, as elsewhere, there is much current and proposed legislation that gives cause for concern from the point of view of morality, and the Catholic community, under your guidance, needs to offer a clear and united witness on such matters. Even more important, though, is the gradual opening of the minds and hearts of the wider community to moral truth. Here much remains to be done. Crucial in this regard is the role of the lay faithful to act as a "leaven" in society. Yet it cannot be assumed that all Catholic citizens think in harmony with the Church's teaching on today's key ethical questions. Once again, it falls to you to ensure that the moral formation provided at every level of ecclesial life reflects the authentic teaching of the Gospel of life.

In this regard, a matter of deep concern to us all is the state of the family within society. Indeed, Cardinal George mentioned earlier that you have included the strengthening of marriage and family life among the priorities for your attention over the next few years. In this year's "World Day of Peace Message" I spoke of the essential contribution that healthy family life makes to peace within and between nations. In the family home we experience "some of the fundamental elements of peace: justice and love between brothers and sisters, the role of authority expressed by parents, loving concern for the members who are weaker because of youth, sickness or old age, mutual help in the necessities of life, readiness to accept others and, if necessary, to forgive them" (no. 3). The family is also the primary place for evangelization, for passing on the faith, for helping young people to appreciate the importance of religious practice and Sunday observance. How can we not be dismayed as we observe the sharp decline of the family as a basic element of Church and society? Divorce and infidelity have increased, and many young men and women are choosing to postpone marriage or to forego it altogether. To some young Catholics, the sacramental bond of marriage seems scarcely distinguishable from a civil bond, or even a purely informal and open-ended arrangement to live with another person. Hence we have an alarming decrease in the number of Catholic marriages in the United States together with an increase in cohabitation, in which the Christ-like mutual self-giving of spouses, sealed by a public promise to live out the demands of an indissoluble lifelong commitment, is simply absent. In such circumstances, children are denied the secure environment that they need in order truly to flourish as human beings, and society is denied the stable building blocks which it requires if the cohesion and moral focus of the community are to be maintained.

As my predecessor, Pope John Paul II, taught, "The person principally responsible in the diocese for the pastoral care of the family is the bishop ... he must devote to it personal interest, care, time, personnel and resources, but above all personal support for the families and for all those who ... assist him in the pastoral care of the family" (*Familiaris Consortio*, 73). It is your task to proclaim boldly the arguments from faith and reason in favor of the institution of marriage, understood as a lifelong commitment between a man and a woman, open to the transmission of life. This message should resonate with people today, because it is essentially an unconditional and unreserved "yes" to life, a "yes" to love, and a "yes" to the aspirations at the heart of our common humanity, as we strive to fulfill our deep yearning for intimacy with others and with the Lord.

Among the countersigns to the gospel of life found in America and elsewhere is one that causes deep shame: the sexual abuse of minors. Many of you have spoken to me of the enormous pain that your communities have suffered when clerics have betrayed their priestly obligations and duties by such gravely immoral behavior. As you strive to eliminate this evil wherever it occurs, you may be assured of the prayerful support of God's people throughout the world. Rightly, you attach priority to showing compassion and care to the victims. It is your God-given responsibility as pastors to bind up the wounds caused by every breach of trust, to foster healing, to promote reconciliation and to reach out with loving concern to those so seriously wronged.

Responding to this situation has not been easy and, as the President of your Episcopal Conference has indicated, it was "sometimes very badly handled." Now that the scale and gravity of the problem is more clearly understood, you have been able to adopt more focused remedial and disciplinary measures and to promote a safe environment that gives greater protection to young people. While it must be remembered that the overwhelming majority of clergy and religious in America do outstanding work in bringing the liberating message of the Gospel to the people entrusted to their care, it is vitally important that the vulnerable always be shielded from those who would cause harm. In this regard, your efforts to heal and protect are bearing great fruit not only for those directly under your pastoral care, but for all of society.

If they are to achieve their full purpose, however, the policies and programs you have adopted need to be placed in a wider context. Children deserve to grow up with a healthy understanding of sexuality and its proper place in human relationships. They should be spared the degrading manifestations and the crude manipulation of sexuality so prevalent today. They have a right to be educated in authentic moral values rooted in the dignity of the human person. This brings us back to our consideration of the centrality of the family and the need to promote the Gospel of life. What does it mean to speak of child protection when pornography and violence can be viewed in so many homes through media widely available today? We need to reassess urgently the values underpinning society, so that a sound moral formation can be offered to young people and adults alike. All have a part to play in this task — not only parents, religious leaders, teachers and catechists, but the media and entertainment industries as well. Indeed, every member of society can contribute to this moral renewal and benefit from it. Truly caring about young people and the future of our civilization means recognizing our responsibility to promote and live by the authentic moral values which alone enable the human person to flourish. It falls to you as pastors modelled upon Christ, the Good Shepherd, to proclaim this message loud and clear, and thus to address the sin of abuse within the wider context of sexual *mores*. Moreover, by acknowledging and confronting the problem when it occurs in an ecclesial setting, you can give a lead to others, since this scourge is found not only within your dioceses, but in every sector of society. It calls for a determined, collective response.

Priests, too, need your guidance and closeness during this difficult time. They have experienced shame over what has occurred, and there are those who feel they have lost some of the trust and esteem they once enjoyed. Not a few are experiencing a closeness to Christ in his Passion as they struggle to come to terms with the consequences of the crisis. The bishop, as father, brother and friend of his priests, can help them to draw spiritual fruit from this union with Christ by making them aware of the Lord's consoling presence in the midst of their suffering, and by encouraging them to walk with the Lord along the path of hope (cf. *Spe Salvi*, 39). As Pope John Paul II observed six years ago, "we must be confident that this time of trial will bring a purification of the entire Catholic community," leading to "a holier priesthood, a holier episcopate and a holier Church" ("Address to the Cardinals of the United States," April 23, 2002, 4). There are many signs that, during the intervening period, such purification has indeed been taking place. Christ's abiding presence in the midst of our suffering is gradually transforming our darkness into light: all things are indeed being made new in Christ Jesus our hope.

At this stage a vital part of your task is to strengthen relationships with your clergy, especially in those cases where tension has arisen between priests and their bishops in the wake of the crisis. It is important that you continue to show them your concern, to support them, and to lead by example. In this way you will surely help them to encounter the living God, and point them towards the life-transforming hope of which the Gospel speaks. If you yourselves live in a manner closely configured to Christ, the Good Shepherd, who laid down his life for his sheep, you will inspire your brother priests to rededicate themselves to the service of their flocks with Christ-like generosity. Indeed a clearer focus upon the imitation of Christ in holiness of life is exactly what is needed in order for us to move forward. We need to rediscover the joy of living a Christ-centered life, cultivating the virtues, and immersing ourselves in prayer. When the faithful know that their pastor is a man who prays and who dedicates his life to serving them, they respond with warmth and affection which nourishes and sustains the life of the whole community.

Time spent in prayer is never wasted, however urgent the duties that press upon us from every side. Adoration of Christ our Lord in the Blessed Sacrament prolongs and intensifies the union with him that is established through the Eucharistic celebration (cf. *Sacramentum Caritatis*, 66). Contemplation of the mysteries of the Rosary releases all their saving power and it conforms, unites and consecrates us to Jesus Christ (cf. *Rosarium Virginis Mariae*, 11, 15). Fidelity to the Liturgy of the Hours ensures that the whole of our day is sanctified and it continually reminds us of the need to remain focused on doing God's work, however many pressures and distractions may arise from the task at hand. Thus our devotion helps us to speak and act *in persona Christi*, to teach, govern and sanctify the faithful in the name of Jesus, to bring his reconciliation, his healing and his love to all his beloved brothers and sisters. This radical configuration to Christ, the Good Shepherd, lies at the heart of our pastoral ministry, and if we open ourselves through prayer to the power of the Spirit, he will give us the gifts we need to carry out our daunting task, so that we need never "be anxious how to speak or what to say" (Mt 10:19).

As I conclude my words to you this evening, I commend the Church in your country most particularly to the maternal care and intercession of Mary Immaculate, Patroness of the United States. May she who carried within her womb the hope of all the nations intercede for the people of this country, so that all may be made new in Jesus Christ her Son. My dear Brother Bishops, I assure each of you here present of my deep friendship and my participation in your pastoral concerns. To all of you, and to your clergy, religious and lay faithful, I cordially impart my Apostolic Blessing as a pledge of joy and peace in the Risen Lord.

MEETING WITH THE BISHOPS OF THE UNITED STATES OF AMERICA

RESPONSES OF HIS HOLINESS BENEDICT XVI TO THE QUESTIONS POSED BY THE BISHOPS

National Shrine of the Immaculate Conception in Washington, DC. Wednesday, April 16, 2008

---

1. The Holy Father is asked to give his assessment of the challenge of increasing secularism in public life and relativism in intellectual life, and his advice on how to confront these challenges pastorally and evangelize more effectively.

I touched upon this theme briefly in my address. It strikes me as significant that here in America, unlike many places in Europe, the secular mentality has not been intrinsically opposed to religion. Within the context of the separation of Church and State, American society has always been marked by a fundamental respect for religion and its public role, and, if polls are to be believed, the American people are deeply religious. But it is not enough to count on this traditional religiosity and go about business as usual, even as its foundations are being slowly undermined. A serious commitment to evangelization cannot prescind from a profound diagnosis of the real challenges the Gospel encounters in contemporary American culture.

Of course, what is essential is a correct understanding of the just autonomy of the secular order, an autonomy which cannot be divorced from God the Creator and his saving plan (cf. *Gaudium et Spes*, 36). Perhaps America's brand of secularism poses a particular problem: it allows for professing belief in God, and respects the public role of religion and the Churches, but at the same time it can subtly reduce religious belief to a lowest common denominator. Faith becomes a passive acceptance that certain things "out there" are true, but without practical relevance for everyday life. The result is a growing separation of faith from life: living "as if God did not exist." This is aggravated by an individualistic and eclectic approach to faith and religion: far from a Catholic approach to "thinking with the Church," each person believes he or she has a right to pick and choose, maintaining external social bonds but without an integral, interior conversion to the law of Christ. Consequently, rather than being transformed and renewed in mind, Christians are easily tempted to conform themselves to the spirit of this age (cf. Rom 12:3). We have seen this emerge in an acute way in the scandal given by Catholics who promote an alleged right to abortion.

On a deeper level, secularism challenges the Church to reaffirm and to pursue more actively her mission in and to the world. As the Council made clear, the lay faithful have a particular responsibility in this regard. What is needed, I am convinced, is a greater sense of the intrinsic relationship between the Gospel and the natural law on the one hand, and, on the other, the pursuit of authentic human good, as embodied in civil law and in personal moral decisions. In a society that rightly values personal liberty, the Church needs to promote at every level of her teaching – in catechesis, preaching, seminary and university instruction – an apologetics aimed at affirming the truth of Christian revelation, the harmony of faith and reason, and a sound understanding of freedom, seen in positive terms as a liberation both *from* the limitations of sin and *for* an authentic and fulfilling life. In a word, the Gospel has to be preached and taught as an integral way of life, offering an attractive and true answer, intellectually and practically, to real human problems. The "dictatorship of relativism", in the end, is nothing less than a threat to genuine human freedom, which only matures in generosity and fidelity to the truth.

Much more, of course, could be said on this subject: let me conclude, though, by saying that I believe that the Church in America, at this point in her history, is faced with the challenge of recapturing the Catholic vision of reality and presenting it, in an engaging and imaginative way, to a society which markets any number of recipes for human fulfillment. I think in particular of our need to speak to the hearts of young people, who, despite their constant exposure to messages contrary to the Gospel, continue to thirst for authenticity, goodness and truth. Much remains to be done, particularly on the level of preaching and catechesis in parishes and schools, if the new evangelization is to bear fruit for the renewal of ecclesial life in America.

2. The Holy Father is asked about "a certain quiet attrition" by which Catholics are abandoning the practice of the faith, sometimes by an explicit decision, but often by distancing themselves quietly and gradually from attendance at Mass and identification with the Church.

Certainly, much of this has to do with the passing away of a religious culture, sometimes disparagingly referred to as a "ghetto," which reinforced participation and identification with the Church. As I just mentioned, one of the great challenges facing the Church in this country is that of cultivating a Catholic identity which is based not so much on externals as on a way of thinking and acting grounded in the Gospel and enriched by the Church's living tradition.

The issue clearly involves factors such as religious individualism and scandal. Let us go to the heart of the matter: faith cannot survive unless it is nourished, unless it is "formed by charity" (cf. Gal 5:6). Do people today find it difficult to encounter God in our Churches? Has our preaching lost its salt? Might it be that many people have forgotten, or never really learned, how to pray in and with the Church?

Here I am not speaking of people who leave the Church in search of subjective religious "experiences"; this is a pastoral issue which must be addressed on its own terms. I think we are speaking about people who have fallen by the wayside without consciously having rejected their faith in Christ, but, for whatever reason, have not drawn life from the liturgy, the sacraments, preaching. Yet Christian faith, as we know, is essentially ecclesial, and without a living bond to the community, the individual's faith will never grow to maturity. Indeed, to return to the question I just discussed, the result can be a quiet apostasy.

So let me make two brief observations on the problem of "attrition," which I hope will stimulate further reflection.

First, as you know, it is becoming more and more difficult, in our Western societies, to speak in a meaningful way of "salvation." Yet salvation – deliverance from the reality of evil, and the gift of new life and freedom in Christ – is at the heart of the Gospel. We need to discover, as I have suggested, new and engaging ways of proclaiming this message and awakening a thirst for the fulfillment which only Christ can bring. It is in the Church's liturgy, and above all in the sacrament of the Eucharist, that these realities are most powerfully expressed and lived in the life of believers; perhaps we still have much to do in realizing the Council's vision of the liturgy as the exercise of the common priesthood and the impetus for a fruitful apostolate in the world.

Second, we need to acknowledge with concern the almost complete eclipse of an eschatological sense in many of our traditionally Christian societies. As you know, I have pointed to this problem in the encyclical *Spe Salvi*. Suffice it to say that faith and hope are not limited to this world: as theological virtues, they unite us with the Lord and draw us toward the fulfillment not only of our personal destiny but also that of all creation. Faith and hope are the inspiration and basis of our efforts to prepare for the coming of the Kingdom of God. In Christianity there can be no room for purely private religion: Christ is the Savior of the world, and, as members of his Body and sharers in his prophetic, priestly and royal *munera*, we cannot separate our love for him from our commitment to the building up of the Church and the extension of his Kingdom. To the extent that religion becomes a purely private affair, it loses its very soul.

Let me conclude by stating the obvious. The fields are still ripe for harvesting (cf. Jn 4:35); God continues to give the growth (cf. 1 Cor 3:6). We can and must believe, with the late Pope John Paul II, that God is preparing a new springtime for Christianity (cf. *Redemptoris Missio*, 86). What is needed above all, at this time in the history of the Church in America, is a renewal of that apostolic zeal which inspires her shepherds actively to seek out the lost, to bind up those who have been wounded, and to bring strength to those who are languishing (cf. Ez 34:16). And this, as I have said, calls for new ways of thinking based on a sound diagnosis of today's challenges and a commitment to unity in the service of the Church's mission to the present generation.

3. The Holy Father is asked to comment on the decline in vocations despite the growing numbers of the Catholic population, and on the reasons for hope offered by the personal qualities and the thirst for holiness which characterize the candidates who do come forward.

Let us be quite frank: the ability to cultivate vocations to the priesthood and the religious life is a sure sign of the health of a local Church. There is no room for complacency in this regard. God continues to call young people; it is up to all of us to encourage a generous and free response to that call. On the other hand, none of us can take this grace for granted.

In the Gospel, Jesus tells us to pray that the Lord of the harvest will send workers. He even admits that the workers are few in comparison with the abundance of the harvest (cf. Mt 9:37-38). Strange to say, we often think that prayer – the *unum necessarium* – is the one aspect of vocations work which we tend to forget or to undervalue!

Nor am I speaking only of prayer *for vocations*. Prayer itself, born in Catholic families, nurtured by programs of Christian formation, strengthened by the grace of the sacraments, is the first means by which we come to know the Lord's will for our lives. To the extent that we teach young people to pray, and to pray well, we will be cooperating with God's call. Programs, plans and projects have their place; but the discernment of a vocation is above all the fruit of an intimate dialogue between the Lord and his disciples. Young people, if they know how to pray, can be trusted to know what to do with God's call.

It has been noted that there is a growing thirst for holiness in many young people today, and that, although fewer in number, those who come forward show great idealism and much promise. It is important to listen to them, to understand their experiences, and to encourage them to help their peers to see the need for committed priests and religious, as well as the beauty of a life of sacrificial service to the Lord and his Church. To my mind, much is demanded of vocation directors and formators: candidates today, as much as ever, need to be given a sound intellectual and human formation which will enable them not only to respond to the real questions and needs of their contemporaries, but also to mature in their own conversion and to persevere in life-long commitment to their vocation. As bishops, you are conscious of the sacrifice demanded when you are asked to release one of your finest priests for seminary work. I urge you to respond with generosity, for the good of the whole Church.

Finally, I think you know from experience that most of your brother priests are happy in their vocation. What I said in my address about the importance of unity and cooperation within the presbyterate applies here too. There is a need for all of us to move beyond sterile divisions, disagreements and preconceptions, and to listen together to the voice of the Spirit who is guiding the Church into a future of hope. Each of us knows how important priestly fraternity has been in our lives. That fraternity is not only a precious possession, but also an immense resource for the renewal of the priesthood and the raising up of new vocations. I would close by encouraging you to foster opportunities for ever greater dialogue and fraternal encounter among your priests, and especially the younger priests. I am convinced that this will bear great fruit for their own enrichment, for the increase of their love for the priesthood and the Church, and for the effectiveness of their apostolate.

Dear Brother Bishops, with these few observations, I once more encourage all of you in your ministry to the faithful entrusted to your pastoral care, and I commend you to the loving intercession of Mary Immaculate, Mother of the Church.

MEETING WITH THE BISHOPS
OF THE UNITED STATES OF AMERICA

PRESENTATION OF A CHALICE
BY HIS HOLINESS BENEDICT XVI
TO THE ARCHBISHOP OF NEW ORLEANS

National Shrine of the Immaculate Conception in Washington, DC.
Wednesday, April 16, 2008

Before leaving, I would like to pause to acknowledge the immense suffering endured by the people of God in the Archdiocese of New Orleans as a result of Hurricane Katrina, as well as their courage in the challenging work of rebuilding. I would like to present Archbishop Alfred Hughes with a chalice, which I hope will be accepted as a sign of my prayerful solidarity with the faithful of the Archdiocese, and my personal gratitude for the tireless devotion which he and Archbishops Philip Hannan and Francis Schulte showed toward the flock entrusted to their care.

HOLY MASS

HOMILY OF HIS HOLINESS BENEDICT XVI

Washington Nationals Stadium
Thursday, April 17, 2008

Dear Brothers and Sisters in Christ,

"Peace be with you!" (*Jn* 20:19). With these, the first words of the Risen Lord to his disciples, I greet all of you in the joy of this Easter season. Before all else, I thank God for the blessing of being in your midst. I am particularly grateful to Archbishop Wuerl for his kind words of welcome.

Our Mass today brings the Church in the United States back to its roots in nearby Maryland, and commemorates the bicentennial of the first chapter of its remarkable growth – the division by my predecessor, Pope Pius VII, of the original Diocese of Baltimore and the establishment of the Dioceses of Boston, Bardstown (now Louisville), New York and Philadelphia. Two hundred years later, the Church in America can rightfully praise the accomplishment of past generations in bringing together widely differing immigrant groups within the unity of the Catholic faith and in a common commitment to the spread of the Gospel. At the same time, conscious of its rich diversity, the Catholic community in this country has come to appreciate ever more fully the importance of each individual and group offering its own particular gifts to the whole. The Church in the United States is now called to look to the future, firmly grounded in the faith passed on by previous generations, and ready to meet new challenges – challenges no less demanding than those faced by your forebears – with the hope born of God's love, poured into our hearts by the Holy Spirit (cf. *Rom* 5:5).

In the exercise of my ministry as the Successor of Peter, I have come to America to confirm you, my brothers and sisters, in the faith of the Apostles (cf. *Lk* 22:32). I have come to proclaim anew, as Peter proclaimed on the day of Pentecost, that Jesus Christ is Lord and Messiah, risen from the dead, seated in glory at the right hand of the Father, and established as judge of the living and the dead (cf. *Acts* 2:14ff.). I have come to repeat the Apostle's urgent call to conversion and the forgiveness of sins, and to implore from the Lord a new outpouring of the Holy Spirit upon the Church in this country. As we have heard throughout this Easter season, the Church was born of the Spirit's gift of repentance and faith in the risen Lord. In every age she is impelled by the same Spirit to bring to men and women of every race, language and people (cf. *Rev* 5:9) the good news of our reconciliation with God in Christ.

The readings of today's Mass invite us to consider the growth of the Church in America as one chapter in the greater story of the Church's expansion following the descent of the Holy Spirit at Pentecost. In those readings we see the inseparable link between the risen Lord, the gift of the Spirit for the forgiveness of sins, and the mystery of the Church. Christ established his Church on the foundation of the Apostles (cf. Rev 21:14) as a visible, structured community which is at the same time a spiritual communion, a mystical body enlivened by the Spirit's manifold gifts, and the sacrament of salvation for all humanity (cf. *Lumen Gentium*, 8). In every time and place, the Church is called to grow in unity through constant conversion to Christ, whose saving work is proclaimed by the successors of the Apostles and celebrated in the sacraments. This unity, in turn, gives rise to an unceasing missionary outreach, as the Spirit spurs believers to proclaim "the great works of God" and to invite all people to enter the community of those saved by the blood of Christ and granted new life in his Spirit.

I pray, then, that this significant anniversary in the life of the Church in the United States, and the presence of the Successor of Peter in your midst, will be an occasion for all Catholics to reaffirm their unity in the apostolic faith, to offer their contemporaries a convincing account of the hope which inspires them (cf. 1 Pet 3:15), and to be renewed in missionary zeal for the extension of God's Kingdom.

The world needs this witness! Who can deny that the present moment is a crossroads, not only for the Church in America but also for society as a whole? It is a time of great promise, as we see the human family in many ways drawing closer together and becoming ever more interdependent. Yet at the same time we see clear signs of a disturbing breakdown in the very foundations of society: signs of alienation, anger and polarization on the part of many of our contemporaries; increased violence; a weakening of the moral sense; a coarsening of social relations; and a growing forgetfulness of Christ and God. The Church, too, sees signs of immense promise in her many strong parishes and vital movements, in the enthusiasm for the faith shown by so many young people, in the number of those who each year embrace the Catholic faith, and in a greater interest in prayer and catechesis. At the same time she senses, often painfully, the presence of division and polarization in her midst, as well as the troubling realization that many of the baptized, rather than acting as a spiritual leaven in the world, are inclined to embrace attitudes contrary to the truth of the Gospel.

"Lord, send out your Spirit, and renew the face of the earth!" (cf. Ps 104:30). The words of today's Responsorial Psalm are a prayer which rises up from the heart of the Church in every time and place. They remind us that the Holy Spirit has been poured out as the first fruits of a new creation, "new heavens and a new earth" (cf. 2 Pet 3:13; Rev 21:1), in which God's peace will reign and the human family will be reconciled in justice and love. We have heard Saint Paul tell us that all creation is even now "groaning" in expectation of that true freedom which is God's gift to his children (Rom 8:21-22), a freedom which enables us to live in conformity to his will. Today let us pray fervently that the Church in America will be renewed in that same Spirit, and sustained in her mission of proclaiming the Gospel to a world that longs for genuine freedom (cf. Jn 8:32), authentic happiness, and the fulfillment of its deepest aspirations!

Here I wish to offer a special word of gratitude and encouragement to all those who have taken up the challenge of the Second Vatican Council, so often reiterated by Pope John Paul II, and committed their lives to the new evangelization. I thank my brother bishops, priests and deacons, men and women religious, parents, teachers and catechists. The fidelity and courage with which the Church in this country will respond to the challenges raised by an increasingly secular and materialistic culture will depend in large part upon your own fidelity in handing on the treasure of our Catholic faith. Young people need to be helped to discern the path that leads to true freedom: the path of a sincere and generous imitation of Christ, the path of commitment to justice and peace. Much progress has been made in developing solid programs of catechesis, yet so much more remains to be done in forming the hearts and minds of the young in knowledge and love of the Lord. The challenges confronting us require a comprehensive and sound instruction in the truths of the faith. But they also call for cultivating a mindset, an intellectual "culture," which is genuinely Catholic, confident in the profound harmony of faith and reason, and prepared to bring the richness of faith's vision to bear on the urgent issues which affect the future of American society.

Dear friends, my visit to the United States is meant to be a witness to "Christ our Hope." Americans have always been a people of hope: your ancestors came to this country with the expectation of finding new freedom and opportunity, while the vastness of the unexplored wilderness inspired in them the hope of being able to start completely anew, building a new nation on new foundations. To be sure, this promise was not experienced by all the inhabitants of this land; one thinks of the injustices endured by the native American peoples and by those brought here forcibly from Africa as slaves. Yet hope, hope for the future, is very much a part of the American character. And the Christian virtue of hope – the hope poured into our hearts by the Holy Spirit, the hope which supernaturally purifies and corrects our aspirations by focusing them on the Lord and his saving plan – that hope has also marked, and continues to mark, the life of the Catholic community in this country.

It is in the context of this hope born of God's love and fidelity that I acknowledge the pain which the Church in America has experienced as a result of the sexual abuse of minors. No words of mine could describe the pain and harm inflicted by such abuse. It is important that those who have suffered be given loving pastoral attention. Nor can I adequately describe the damage that has occurred within the community of the Church. Great efforts have already been made to deal honestly and fairly with this tragic situation, and to ensure that children – whom our Lord loves so deeply (cf. Mk 10:14), and who are our greatest treasure – can grow up in a safe environment. These efforts to protect children must continue. Yesterday I spoke with your bishops about this. Today I encourage each of you to do what you can to foster healing and reconciliation, and to assist those who have been hurt. Also, I ask you to love your priests, and to affirm them in the excellent work that they do. And above all, pray that the Holy Spirit will pour out his gifts upon the Church, the gifts that lead to conversion, forgiveness and growth in holiness.

Saint Paul speaks, as we heard in the second reading, of a kind of prayer which arises from the depths of our hearts in sighs too deep for words, in "groanings" (Rom 8:26) inspired by the Spirit. This is prayer which yearns, in the midst of chastisement, for the fulfillment of God's promises. It is a prayer of unfailing hope, but also one of patient endurance and, often, accompanied by suffering for the truth. Through this prayer, we share in the mystery of Christ's own weakness and suffering, while trusting firmly in the victory of his Cross. With this prayer, may the Church in America embrace ever more fully the way of conversion and fidelity to the demands of the Gospel. And may all Catholics experience the consolation of hope, and the Spirit's gifts of joy and strength.

In today's Gospel, the risen Lord bestows the gift of the Holy Spirit upon the Apostles and grants them the authority to forgive sins. Through the surpassing power of Christ's grace, entrusted to frail human ministers, the Church is constantly reborn and each of us is given the hope of a new beginning. Let us trust in the Spirit's power to inspire conversion, to heal every wound, to overcome every division, and to inspire new life and freedom. How much we need these gifts! And how close at hand they are, particularly in the sacrament of Penance! The liberating power of this sacrament, in which our honest confession of sin is met by God's merciful word of pardon and peace, needs to be rediscovered and reappropriated by every Catholic. To a great extent, the renewal of the Church in America and throughout the world depends on the renewal of the practice of Penance and the growth in holiness which that sacrament both inspires and accomplishes.

"In hope we were saved!" (Rom 8:24). As the Church in the United States gives thanks for the blessings of the past two hundred years, I invite you, your families, and every parish and religious community, to trust in the power of grace to create a future of promise for God's people in this country. I ask you, in the Lord Jesus, to set aside all division and to work with joy to prepare a way for him, in fidelity to his word and in constant conversion to his will. Above all, I urge you to continue to be a leaven of evangelical hope in American society, striving to bring the light and truth of the Gospel to the task of building an ever more just and free world for generations yet to come.

Those who have hope must live different lives! (cf. *Spe Salvi*, 2). By your prayers, by the witness of your faith, by the fruitfulness of your charity, may you point the way towards that vast horizon of hope which God is even now opening up to his Church, and indeed to all humanity: the vision of a world reconciled and renewed in Christ Jesus, our Savior. To him be all honor and glory, now and forever. Amen!

MEETING WITH CATHOLIC EDUCATORS

ADDRESS OF HIS HOLINESS BENEDICT XVI

Conference Hall of the Catholic University of America in Washington, DC.
Thursday, April 17, 2008

Your Eminences,
Dear Brother Bishops,
Distinguished Professors, Teachers and Educators,

"How beautiful are the footsteps of those who bring good news" (Rom 10:15-17). With these words of Isaiah quoted by Saint Paul, I warmly greet each of you – bearers of wisdom – and through you the staff, students and families of the many and varied institutions of learning that you represent. It is my great pleasure to meet you and to share with you some thoughts regarding the nature and identity of Catholic education today. I especially wish to thank Father David O'Connell, President and Rector of the Catholic University of America. Your kind words of welcome are much appreciated. Please extend my heartfelt gratitude to the entire community – faculty, staff and students – of this University.

Education is integral to the mission of the Church to proclaim the Good News. First and foremost every Catholic educational institution is a place to encounter the living God who in Jesus Christ reveals his transforming love and truth (cf. *Spe Salvi*, 4). This relationship elicits a desire to grow in the knowledge and understanding of Christ and his teaching. In this way those who meet him are drawn by the very power of the Gospel to lead a new life characterized by all that is beautiful, good, and true; a life of Christian witness nurtured and strengthened within the community of our Lord's disciples, the Church.

The dynamic between personal encounter, knowledge and Christian witness is integral to the *diakonia* of truth which the Church exercises in the midst of humanity. God's revelation offers every generation the opportunity to discover the ultimate truth about its own life and the goal of history. This task is never easy; it involves the entire Christian community and motivates each generation of Christian educators to ensure that the power of God's truth permeates every dimension of the institutions they serve. In this way, Christ's Good News is set to work, guiding both teacher and student towards the objective truth which, in transcending the particular and the subjective, points to the universal and absolute that enables us to proclaim with confidence the hope which does not disappoint (cf. Rom 5:5). Set against personal struggles, moral confusion and fragmentation of knowledge, the noble goals of scholarship and education, founded on the unity of truth and in service of the person and the community, become an especially powerful instrument of hope.

Dear friends, the history of this nation includes many examples of the Church's commitment in this regard. The Catholic community here has in fact made education one of its highest priorities. This undertaking has not come without great sacrifice. Towering figures, like Saint Elizabeth Ann Seton and other founders and foundresses, with great tenacity and foresight, laid the foundations of what is today a remarkable network of parochial schools contributing to the spiritual well-being of the Church and the nation. Some, like Saint Katharine Drexel, devoted their lives to educating those whom others had neglected – in her case, African Americans and Native Americans. Countless dedicated religious sisters, brothers, and priests together with selfless parents have, through Catholic schools, helped generations of immigrants to rise from poverty and take their place in mainstream society.

This sacrifice continues today. It is an outstanding apostolate of hope, seeking to address the material, intellectual and spiritual needs of over three million children and students. It also provides a highly commendable opportunity for the entire Catholic community to contribute generously to the financial needs of our institutions. Their long-term sustainability must be assured. Indeed, everything possible must be during the national feast of Thanksgiving, joint initiatives in charitable activities, a shared voice on important public issues: these are some ways in which members of different religions come together to enhance mutual understanding and promote the common good. I encourage all religious groups in America to persevere in their collaboration and thus enrich public life with the spiritual values that motivate your action in the world.

The place where we are now gathered was founded specifically for promoting this type of collaboration. Indeed, the Pope John Paul II Cultural Center seeks to offer a Christian voice to the "human search for meaning and purpose in life" in a world of "varied religious, ethnic and cultural communities" (*Mission Statement*). This institution reminds us of this nation's conviction that all people should be free to pursue happiness in a way consonant with their nature as creatures endowed with reason and free will.

Americans have always valued the ability to worship freely and in accordance with their conscience. Alexis de Tocqueville, the French historian and observer of American affairs, was fascinated with this aspect of the nation. He remarked that this is a country in which religion and freedom are "intimately linked" in contributing to a stable democracy that fosters social virtues and participation in the communal life of all its citizens. In urban areas, it is common for individuals from different cultural backgrounds and religions to engage with one another daily in commercial, social and educational settings. Today, in classrooms throughout the country, young Christians, Jews, Muslims, Hindus, Buddhists, and indeed children of all religions sit side-by-side, learning with one another and from one another. This diversity gives rise to new challenges that spark a deeper reflection on the core principles of a democratic society. May others take heart from your experience, realizing that a united society can indeed arise from a plurality of peoples – "*E pluribus unum*": "out of many, one" – provided that all recognize religious liberty as a basic civil right (cf. *Dignitatis Humanae*, 2).

The task of upholding religious freedom is never completed. New situations and challenges invite citizens and leaders to reflect on how their decisions respect this basic human right. Protecting religious freedom within the rule of law does not guarantee that peoples – particularly minorities – will be spared from unjust forms of discrimination and prejudice. This requires constant effort on the part of all members of society to ensure that citizens are afforded the opportunity to worship peaceably and to pass on their religious heritage to their children.

The transmission of religious traditions to succeeding generations not only helps to preserve a heritage; it also sustains and nourishes the surrounding culture in the present day. The same holds true for dialogue between religions; both the participants and society are enriched. As we grow in understanding of one another, we see that we share an esteem for ethical values, discernable to human reason, which are revered by all peoples of goodwill. The world begs for a common witness to these values. I therefore invite all religious people to view dialogue not only as a means of enhancing mutual understanding, but also as a way of serving society at large. By bearing witness to those moral truths which they hold in common with all men and women of goodwill, religious groups will exert a positive influence on the wider culture, and inspire neighbors, co-workers and fellow citizens to join in

the task of strengthening the ties of solidarity. In the words of President Franklin Delano Roosevelt: "no greater thing could come to our land today than a revival of the spirit of faith."

A concrete example of the contribution religious communities make to civil society is faith-based schools. These institutions enrich children both intellectually and spiritually. Led by their teachers to discover the divinely bestowed dignity of each human being, young people learn to respect the beliefs and practices of others, thus enhancing a nation's civic life.

What an enormous responsibility religious leaders have: to imbue society with a profound awe and respect for human life and freedom; to ensure that human dignity is recognized and cherished; to facilitate peace and justice; to teach children what is right, good and reasonable!

There is a further point I wish to touch upon here. I have noticed a growing interest among governments to sponsor programs intended to promote interreligious and intercultural dialogue. These are praiseworthy initiatives. At the same time, religious freedom, interreligious dialogue and faith-based education aim at something more than a consensus regarding ways to implement practical strategies for advancing peace. The broader purpose of dialogue is to discover the truth. What is the origin and destiny of mankind? What are good and evil? What awaits us at the end of our earthly existence? Only by addressing these deeper questions can we build a solid basis for the peace and security of the human family, for "wherever and whenever men and women are enlightened by the splendor of truth, they naturally set out on the path of peace" (*Message for the 2006 World Day of Peace*, 3).

We are living in an age when these questions are too often marginalized. Yet they can never be erased from the human heart. Throughout history, men and women have striven to articulate their restlessness with this passing world. In the Judeo-Christian tradition, the Psalms are full of such expressions: "My spirit is overwhelmed within me" (Ps 143:4; cf. Ps 6:6; 31:10; 32:3; 38:8; 77:3); "why are you cast down, my soul, why groan within me?" (Ps 42:5). The response is always one of faith: "Hope in God, I will praise him still; my Savior and my God" (Ps 42:5, 11; cf. Ps 43:5; 62:5). Spiritual leaders have a special duty, and we might say competence, to place the deeper questions at the forefront of human consciousness, to reawaken mankind to the mystery of human existence, and to make space in a frenetic world for reflection and prayer.

Confronted with these deeper questions concerning the origin and destiny of mankind, Christianity proposes Jesus of Nazareth. He, we believe, is the eternal *Logos* who became flesh in order to reconcile man to God and reveal the underlying reason of all things. It is he whom we bring to the forum of interreligious dialogue. The ardent desire to follow in his footsteps spurs Christians to open their minds and hearts in dialogue (cf. Lk 10:25-37; Jn 4:7-26).

Dear friends, in our attempt to discover points of commonality, perhaps we have shied away from the responsibility to discuss our differences with calmness and clarity. While always uniting our hearts and minds in the call for peace, we must also listen attentively to the voice of truth. In this way, our dialogue will not stop at identifying a common set of values, but go on to probe their ultimate foundation. We have reason to fear, for the truth unveils for us the essential relationship etween the world and God. We are able to perceive that peace is "heavenly gift" that calls us to conform human history to the divine der. Herein lies the "truth of peace" (cf. *Message for the 2006 World ay of Peace*).

As we have seen then, the higher goal of interreligious dialogue quires a clear exposition of our respective religious tenets. In this gard, colleges, universities and study centers are important forums for candid exchange of religious ideas. The Holy See, for its part, seeks carry forward this important work through the Pontifical Council for erreligious Dialogue, the Pontifical Institute for Arabic and Islamic udies, and various Pontifical Universities.

Dear friends, let our sincere dialogue and cooperation inspire all eople to ponder the deeper questions of their origin and destiny. May e followers of all religions stand together in defending and promoting e and religious freedom everywhere. By giving ourselves generously this sacred task − through dialogue and countless small acts of love, derstanding and compassion − we can be instruments of peace for e whole human family.

Peace upon you all!

EETING WITH REPRESENTATIVES
F THE JEWISH COMMUNITY

ORDS OF HIS HOLINESS BENEDICT XVI

otunda" Hall of the Pope John Paul II Cultural Center
Washington, DC.
ursday, April 17, 2008

y *dear friends*,

I extend special greetings of peace to the Jewish community in the ited States and throughout the world as you prepare to celebrate the nual feast of *Pesah*. My visit to this country has coincided with this st, allowing me to meet with you personally and to assure you of my ayers as you recall the signs and wonders God performed in liberat g his chosen people. Motivated by our common spiritual heritage, I n pleased to entrust to you *this message* as a testimony to our hope ntered on the Almighty and his mercy.

EETING WITH THE MEMBERS OF THE GENERAL ASSEMBLY
F THE UNITED NATIONS ORGANIZATION

DDRESS OF HIS HOLINESS BENEDICT XVI

ew York
iday, April 18, 2008

r. President,
dies and Gentlemen,

As I begin my address to this Assembly, I would like first of all to express to you, Mr. President, my sincere gratitude for your kind words. My thanks go also to the Secretary-General, Mr. Ban Ki-moon, for inviting me to visit the headquarters of this Organization and for the welcome that he has extended to me. I greet the Ambassadors and Diplomats from the Member States, and all those present. Through you, I greet the peoples who are represented here. They look to this institution to carry forward the founding inspiration to establish a "centre for harmonizing the actions of nations in the attainment of these common ends" of peace and development (cf. *Charter of the United Nations*, article 1.2-1.4). As Pope John Paul II expressed it in 1995, the Organization should be "a moral centre where all the nations of the world feel at home and develop a shared awareness of being, as it were, a 'family of nations'" (*Address to the General Assembly of the United Nations on the 50th Anniversary of its Foundation*, New York, 5 October 1995, 14).

Through the United Nations, States have established universal objectives which, even if they do not coincide with the total common good of the human family, undoubtedly represent a fundamental part of that good. The founding principles of the Organization − the desire for peace, the quest for justice, respect for the dignity of the person, humanitarian cooperation and assistance − express the just aspirations of the human spirit, and constitute the ideals which should underpin international relations. As my predecessors Paul VI and John Paul II have observed from this very podium, all this is something that the Catholic Church and the Holy See follow attentively and with interest, seeing in your activity an example of how issues and conflicts concerning the world community can be subject to common regulation. The United Nations embodies the aspiration for a "greater degree of international ordering" (John Paul II, *Sollicitudo Rei Socialis*, 43), inspired and governed by the principle of subsidiarity, and therefore capable of responding to the demands of the human family through binding international rules and through structures capable of harmonizing the day-to-day unfolding of the lives of peoples. This is all the more necessary at a time when we experience the obvious paradox of a multilateral consensus that continues to be in crisis because it is still subordinated to the decisions of a few, whereas the world's problems call for interventions in the form of collective action by the international community.

Indeed, questions of security, development goals, reduction of local and global inequalities, protection of the environment, of resources and of the climate, require all international leaders to act jointly and to show a readiness to work in good faith, respecting the law, and promoting solidarity with the weakest regions of the planet. I am thinking especially of those countries in Africa and other parts of the world which remain on the margins of authentic integral development, and are therefore at risk of experiencing only the negative effects of globalization. In the context of international relations, it is necessary to recognize the higher role played by rules and structures that are intrinsically ordered to promote the common good, and therefore to safeguard human freedom. These regulations do not limit freedom. On the contrary, they promote it when they prohibit behavior and actions which work against the common good, curb its effective exercise and hence compromise the dignity of every human person. In the name of freedom, there has to be a correlation between rights and duties, by which every person is called to assume responsibility for his or her choices, made as a consequence of entering into relations with others. Here our thoughts turn also to the way the results of scientific research and technological advances have sometimes been applied. Notwithstanding the enormous benefits that humanity can gain, some instances of this represent a clear violation of the order of creation, to the point where not only is the sacred character of life contradicted, but the human person and the family are robbed of their natural identity. Likewise, international action to preserve the environment and to protect various forms of life on earth must not only guarantee a rational use of technology and science, but must also rediscover the authentic image of creation. This never requires a choice to be made between science and ethics: rather it is a question of adopting a scientific method that is truly respectful of ethical imperatives.

Recognition of the unity of the human family, and attention to the innate dignity of every man and woman, today find renewed emphasis in the principle of the responsibility to protect. This has only recently been defined, but it was already present implicitly at the origins of the United Nations, and is now increasingly characteristic of its activity. Every State has the primary duty to protect its own population from grave and sustained violations of human rights, as well as from the consequences of humanitarian crises, whether natural or man-made. If States are unable to guarantee such protection, the international community must intervene with the juridical means provided in the United Nations Charter and in other international instruments. The action of the international community and its institutions, provided that it respects the principles undergirding the international order, should never be interpreted as an unwarranted imposition or a limitation of sovereignty. On the contrary, it is indifference or failure to intervene that do the real damage. What is needed is a deeper search for ways of pre-empting and managing conflicts by exploring every possible diplomatic avenue, and giving attention and encouragement to even the faintest sign of dialogue or desire for reconciliation.

The principle of "responsibility to protect" was considered by the ancient *ius gentium* as the foundation of every action taken by those in government with regard to the governed: at the time when the concept of national sovereign States was first developing, the Dominican Friar Francisco de Vitoria, rightly considered as a precursor of the idea of the United Nations, described this responsibility as an aspect of natural reason shared by all nations, and the result of an international order whose task it was to regulate relations between peoples. Now, as then, this principle has to invoke the idea of the person as image of the Creator, the desire for the absolute and the essence of freedom. The founding of the United Nations, as we know, coincided with the profound upheavals that humanity experienced when reference to the meaning of transcendence and natural reason was abandoned, and in consequence, freedom and human dignity were grossly violated. When this happens, it threatens the objective foundations of the values inspiring and governing the international order and it undermines the cogent and inviolable principles formulated and consolidated by the United Nations. When faced with new and insistent challenges, it is a mistake to fall back on a pragmatic approach, limited to determining "common ground," minimal in content and weak in its effect.

This reference to human dignity, which is the foundation and goal of the responsibility to protect, leads us to the theme we are specifically focusing upon this year, which marks the sixtieth anniversary of the *Universal Declaration of Human Rights*. This document was the outcome of a convergence of different religious and cultural traditions, all of them motivated by the common desire to place the human person at the head of institutions, laws and the workings of society, and to consider the human person essential for the world of culture, religion and science. Human rights are increasingly being presented as the common language and the ethical substratum of international relations. At the same time, the universality, indivisibility and interdependence of human rights all serve as guarantees safeguarding human dignity. It is evident, though, that the rights recognized and expounded in the *Declaration* apply to everyone by virtue of the common origin of the person, who remains the high-point of God's creative design for the world and for history. They are based on the natural law inscribed on human hearts and present in different cultures and civilizations. Removing human rights from this context would mean restricting their range and yielding to a relativistic conception, according to which the meaning and interpretation of rights could vary and their universality would be denied in the name of different cultural, political, social and even religious outlooks. This great variety of viewpoints must not be allowed to obscure the fact that not only rights are universal, but so too is the human person, the subject of those rights.

The life of the community, both domestically and internationally, clearly demonstrates that respect for rights, and the guarantees that follow from them, are measures of the common good that serve to evaluate the relationship between justice and injustice, development and poverty, security and conflict. The promotion of human rights remains the most effective strategy for eliminating inequalities between countries and social groups, and for increasing security. Indeed, the victims of hardship and despair, whose human dignity is violated with impunity, become easy prey to the call to violence, and they can then become violators of peace. The common good that human rights help to accomplish cannot, however, be attained merely by applying correct procedures, nor even less by achieving a balance between competing rights. The merit of the *Universal Declaration* is that it has enabled different cultures, juridical expressions and institutional models to converge around a fundamental nucleus of values, and hence of rights. Today, though, efforts need to be redoubled in the face of pressure to reinterpret the foundations of the *Declaration* and to compromise its inner unity so as to facilitate a move away from the protection of human dignity towards the satisfaction of simple interests, often particular interests. The *Declaration* was adopted as a "common standard of achievement" (*Preamble*) and cannot be applied piecemeal, according to trends or selective choices that merely run the risk of contradicting the unity of the human person and thus the indivisibility of human rights.

Experience shows that legality often prevails over justice when the insistence upon rights makes them appear as the exclusive result of legislative enactments or normative decisions taken by the various agencies of those in power. When presented purely in terms of legality, rights risk becoming weak propositions divorced from the ethical and rational dimension which is their foundation and their goal. The *Universal Declaration*, rather, has reinforced the conviction that respect for human rights is principally rooted in unchanging justice, on which the binding force of international proclamations is also based. This aspect is often overlooked when the attempt is made to deprive rights of their true function in the name of a narrowly utilitarian perspective. Since rights and the resulting duties follow naturally from human interaction, it is easy to forget that they are the fruit of a commonly held sense of justice built primarily upon solidarity among the members of society.

nd hence valid at all times and for all peoples. This intuition was xpressed as early as the fifth century by Augustine of Hippo, one of e masters of our intellectual heritage. He taught that the saying: *Do ot do to others what you would not want done to you* "cannot in any ay vary according to the different understandings that have arisen in e world" (*De Doctrina Christiana*, III, 14). Human rights, then, must e respected as an expression of justice, and not merely because they e enforceable through the will of the legislators.

Ladies and Gentlemen,

As history proceeds, new situations arise, and the attempt is made link them to new rights. Discernment, that is, the capacity to distin-uish good from evil, becomes even more essential in the context of emands that concern the very lives and conduct of persons, com-unities and peoples. In tackling the theme of rights, since important tuations and profound realities are involved, discernment is both an dispensable and a fruitful virtue.

Discernment, then, shows that entrusting exclusively to individual ates, with their laws and institutions, the final responsibility to meet the spirations of persons, communities and entire peoples, can sometimes ave consequences that exclude the possibility of a social order respect- l of the dignity and rights of the person. On the other hand, a vision of e firmly anchored in the religious dimension can help to achieve this, nce recognition of the transcendent value of every man and woman vors conversion of heart, which then leads to a commitment to resist olence, terrorism and war, and to promote justice and peace. This so provides the proper context for the inter-religious dialogue that the nited Nations is called to support, just as it supports dialogue in other eas of human activity. Dialogue should be recognized as the means y which the various components of society can articulate their point of ew and build consensus around the truth concerning particular values goals. It pertains to the nature of religions, freely practiced, that they an autonomously conduct a dialogue of thought and life. If at this vel, too, the religious sphere is kept separate from political action, en great benefits ensue for individuals and communities. On the other nd, the United Nations can count on the results of dialogue between ligions, and can draw fruit from the willingness of believers to place eir experiences at the service of the common good. Their task is to oppose a vision of faith not in terms of intolerance, discrimination and nflict, but in terms of complete respect for truth, coexistence, rights, d reconciliation.

Human rights, of course, must include the right to religious freedom, derstood as the expression of a dimension that is at once individual nd communitarian – a vision that brings out the unity of the person hile clearly distinguishing between the dimension of the citizen and at of the believer. The activity of the United Nations in recent years as ensured that public debate gives space to viewpoints inspired by religious vision in all its dimensions, including ritual, worship, edu-ation, dissemination of information and the freedom to profess and oose religion. It is inconceivable, then, that believers should have suppress a part of themselves – their faith – in order to be active izens. It should never be necessary to deny God in order to enjoy e's rights. The rights associated with religion are all the more in need protection if they are considered to clash with a prevailing secular eology or with majority religious positions of an exclusive nature. The

full guarantee of religious liberty cannot be limited to the free exercise of worship, but has to give due consideration to the public dimension of religion, and hence to the possibility of believers playing their part in building the social order. Indeed, they actually do so, for example through their influential and generous involvement in a vast network of initiatives which extend from Universities, scientific institutions and schools to health care agencies and charitable organizations in the service of the poorest and most marginalized. Refusal to recognize the contribution to society that is rooted in the religious dimension and in the quest for the Absolute – by its nature, expressing communion between persons – would effectively privilege an individualistic ap-proach, and would fragment the unity of the person.

My presence at this Assembly is a sign of esteem for the United Nations, and it is intended to express the hope that the Organization will increasingly serve as a sign of unity between States and an instru-ment of service to the entire human family. It also demonstrates the willingness of the Catholic Church to offer her proper contribution to building international relations in a way that allows every person and every people to feel they can make a difference. In a manner that is consistent with her contribution in the ethical and moral sphere and the free activity of her faithful, the Church also works for the realization of these goals through the international activity of the Holy See. Indeed, the Holy See has always had a place at the assemblies of the Nations, thereby manifesting its specific character as a subject in the interna-tional domain. As the United Nations recently confirmed, the Holy See thereby makes its contribution according to the dispositions of interna-tional law, helps to define that law, and makes appeal to it.

The United Nations remains a privileged setting in which the Church is committed to contributing her experience "of humanity," developed over the centuries among peoples of every race and culture, and plac-ing it at the disposal of all members of the international community. This experience and activity, directed towards attaining freedom for every believer, seeks also to increase the protection given to the rights of the person. Those rights are grounded and shaped by the transcendent nature of the person, which permits men and women to pursue their journey of faith and their search for God in this world. Recognition of this dimension must be strengthened if we are to sustain humanity's hope for a better world and if we are to create the conditions for peace, development, cooperation, and guarantee of rights for future generations.

In my recent encyclical, *Spe Salvi*, I indicated that "every genera-tion has the task of engaging anew in the arduous search for the right way to order human affairs" (no. 25). For Christians, this task is mo-tivated by the hope drawn from the saving work of Jesus Christ. That is why the Church is happy to be associated with the activity of this distinguished Organization, charged with the responsibility of promot-ing peace and good will throughout the earth. Dear Friends, I thank you for this opportunity to address you today, and I promise you of the support of my prayers as you pursue your noble task.

Before I take my leave from this distinguished Assembly, I should like to offer my greetings, in the official languages, to all the Nations here represented.

Peace and Prosperity with God's help!

MEETING WITH THE STAFF
OF THE UNITED NATIONS ORGANIZATION

ADDRESS OF HIS HOLINESS BENEDICT XVI

New York
Friday, April 18, 2008

Ladies and Gentlemen,

Here, within a small space in the busy city of New York, is housed an Organization with a worldwide mission to promote peace and justice. I am reminded of the similar contrast in scale between Vatican City State and the world in which the Church exercises her universal mission and apostolate. The sixteenth-century artists who painted the maps on the walls of the Apostolic Palace reminded the Popes of the vast extent of the known world. In those frescoes, the successors of Peter were offered a tangible sign of the immense outreach of the Church's mission at a time when the discovery of the New World was opening up unforeseen horizons. Here in this glass palace, the art on display has its own way of reminding us of the responsibilities of the United Nations Organization. We see images of the effects of war and poverty, we are reminded of our duty to strive for a better world, and we rejoice in the sheer diversity and exuberance of human culture, manifested in the wide range of peoples and nations gathered together under the umbrella of the international community.

On the occasion of my visit, I wish to pay tribute to the invaluable contribution made by the administrative staff and the many employees of the United Nations, who carry out their duties with such great dedication and professionalism every day – here in New York, in other UN centers, and at special missions all over the world. To you, and to those who have gone before you, I would like to express my personal appreciation and that of the whole Catholic Church. We remember especially the many civilians and peace-keepers who have sacrificed their lives in the field for the good of the peoples they serve – in 2007 alone there were forty-two of them. We also remember the vast multitude who dedicate their lives to work that is never sufficiently acknowledged, often in difficult circumstances. To all of you – translators, secretaries, administrative personnel of every kind, maintenance and security staff, development workers, peace-keepers and many others – thank you, most sincerely. The work that you do makes it possible for the Organization to continue exploring new ways of achieving the goals for which it was founded.

The United Nations is often spoken of as the "family of nations." By the same token, the headquarters here in New York could be described as a home, a place of welcome and concern for the good of family members everywhere. It is an excellent place in which to promote growth in understanding and collaboration between peoples. Rightly, the staff of the United Nations are selected from a wide range of cultures and nationalities. The personnel here constitute a microcosm of the whole world, in which each individual makes an indispensable contribution from the perspective of his or her particular cultural and religious heritage. The ideals that inspired the founders of this institution need to take shape here and in every one of the Organization's missions around the world in the mutual respect and acceptance that are the hallmarks of a thriving family.

In the internal debates of the United Nations, increasing emphas[is] is being placed on the "responsibility to protect." Indeed this is comin[g] to be recognized as the moral basis for a government's claim to autho[r]ity. It is also a feature that naturally appertains to a family, in whic[h] stronger members take care of weaker ones. This Organization pe[r]forms an important service, in the name of the international communit[y] by monitoring the extent to which governments fulfill their responsibili[ty] to protect their citizens. On a day-to-day level, it is you who lay th[e] foundations on which that work is built, by the concern you show f[or] one another in the workplace, and by your solicitude for the man[y] peoples whose needs and aspirations you serve in all that you do.

The Catholic Church, through the international activity of the Ho[ly] See, and through countless initiatives of lay Catholics, local Churche[s] and religious communities, assures you of her support for your work. [I] assure you and your families of a special remembrance in my prayer[s.] May Almighty God bless you always and comfort you with his grac[e] and his peace, so that through the care you offer to the entire huma[n] family, you can continue to be of service to him.

Thank you.

MEETING WITH REPRESENTATIVES
OF THE JEWISH COMMUNITY

WORDS OF HIS HOLINESS BENEDICT XVI

Park East Synagogue, New York
Friday, April 18, 2008

Dear Friends,

Shalom! It is with joy that I come here, just a few hours befo[re] the celebration of your *Pesah*, to express my respect and esteem f[or] the Jewish community in New York City. The proximity of this plac[e] of worship to my residence gives me the opportunity to greet som[e] of you today. I find it moving to recall that Jesus, as a young bo[y] heard the words of Scripture and prayed in a place such as thi[s.] I thank Rabbi Schneier for his words of welcome and I particular[ly] appreciate your kind gift, the spring flowers and the lovely song th[at] the children sang for me. I know that the Jewish community make[s a] valuable contribution to the life of the city, and I encourage all of y[ou] to continue building bridges of friendship with all the many differe[nt] ethnic and religious groups present in your neighborhood. I assu[re] you most especially of my closeness at this time, as you prepare [to] celebrate the great deeds of the Almighty, and to sing the praises [of] Him who has worked such wonders for his people. I would ask tho[se] of you who are present to pass on my greetings and good wish[es] to all the members of the Jewish community. Blessed be the name [of] the Lord!

ECUMENICAL PRAYER SERVICE

ADDRESS OF HIS HOLINESS BENEDICT XVI

St. Joseph's Parish, New York
Friday, April 18, 2008

Dear Brothers and Sisters in Christ,

My heart abounds with gratitude to Almighty God — "the Father of all, who is over all and through all and in all" (Eph 4:6) — for this blessed opportunity to gather with you this evening in prayer. I thank Bishop Dennis Sullivan for his cordial welcome, and I warmly greet all those in attendance representing Christian communities throughout the United States. May the peace of our Lord and Savior be with you all!

Through you, I express my sincere appreciation for the invaluable work of all those engaged in ecumenism: the National Council of Churches, Christian Churches Together, the Catholic Bishops' Secretariat for Ecumenical and Interreligious Affairs, and many others. The contribution of Christians in the United States to the ecumenical movement is felt throughout the world. I encourage all of you to persevere, always relying on the grace of the risen Christ whom we strive to serve by bringing about "the obedience of faith for the sake of his name" (Rom 1:5).

We have just listened to the scriptural passage in which Paul — a "prisoner for the Lord" — delivers his ardent appeal to the members of the Christian community at Ephesus. "I beg you," he writes, "to lead a life worthy of the calling to which you have been called … eager to maintain the unity of the Spirit in the bond of peace" (Eph 4:1-3). Then, after his impassioned litany of unity, Paul reminds his hearers that Jesus, having ascended into heaven, has bestowed upon men and women all the gifts necessary for building up the Body of Christ (cf. Eph 4:11-13).

Paul's exhortation resounds with no less vigor today. His words still in us the confidence that the Lord will never abandon us in our quest for unity. They also call us to live in a way that bears witness to the "one heart and mind" (Acts 4:32), which has always been the distinguishing trait of Christian koinonia (cf. Acts 2:42), and the force drawing others to join the community of believers so that they too might come to share in the "unsearchable riches of Christ" (Eph 3:8; cf. Acts 2:47; 5:14).

Globalization has humanity poised between two poles. On the one hand, there is a growing sense of interconnectedness and interdependency between peoples even when — geographically and culturally speaking — they are far apart. This new situation offers the potential for enhancing a sense of global solidarity and shared responsibility for the well-being of mankind. On the other hand, we cannot deny that the rapid changes occurring in our world also present some disturbing signs of fragmentation and a retreat into individualism. The expanding use of electronic communications has in some cases paradoxically resulted in greater isolation. Many people — including the young — are seeking therefore more authentic forms of community. Also of grave concern is the spread of a secularist ideology that undermines or even rejects transcendent truth. The very possibility of divine revelation, and therefore of Christian faith, is often placed into question by cultural trends widely present in academia, the mass media and public debate. For these reasons, a faithful witness to the Gospel is as urgent as ever. Christians are challenged to give a clear account of the hope that they hold (cf. 1 Pet 3:15).

Too often those who are not Christians, as they observe the splintering of Christian communities, are understandably confused about the Gospel message itself. Fundamental Christian beliefs and practices are sometimes changed within communities by so-called "prophetic actions" that are based on a hermeneutic not always consonant with the datum of Scripture and Tradition. Communities consequently give up the attempt to act as a unified body, choosing instead to function according to the idea of "local options." Somewhere in this process the need for diachronic koinonia — communion with the Church in every age — is lost, just at the time when the world is losing its bearings and needs a persuasive common witness to the saving power of the Gospel (cf. Rom 1:18-23).

Faced with these difficulties, we must first recall that the unity of the Church flows from the perfect oneness of the triune God. In John's Gospel, we are told that Jesus prayed to his Father that his disciples might be one, "just as you are in me and I am in you" (Jn 17:21). This passage reflects the unwavering conviction of the early Christian community that its unity was both caused by, and is reflective of, the unity of the Father, Son, and Holy Spirit. This, in turn, suggests that the internal cohesion of believers was based on the sound integrity of their doctrinal confession (cf. 1 Tim 1:3-11). Throughout the New Testament, we find that the Apostles were repeatedly called to give an account for their faith to both Gentiles (cf. Acts 17:16-34) and Jews (cf. Acts 4:5-22; 5:27-42). The core of their argument was always the historical fact of Jesus' bodily resurrection from the tomb (Acts 2:24, 32; 3:15; 4:10; 5:30; 10.40; 13:30). The ultimate effectiveness of their preaching did not depend on "lofty words" or "human wisdom" (1 Cor 2:13), but rather on the work of the Spirit (Eph 3:5) who confirmed the authoritative witness of the Apostles (cf. 1 Cor 15:1-11). The nucleus of Paul's preaching and that of the early Church was none other than Jesus Christ, and "him crucified" (1 Cor 2:2). But this proclamation had to be guaranteed by the purity of normative doctrine expressed in creedal formulae — symbola — which articulated the essence of the Christian faith and constituted the foundation for the unity of the baptized (cf. 1 Cor 15:3-5; Gal 1:6-9; Unitatis Redintegratio, 2).

My dear friends, the power of the kerygma has lost none of its internal dynamism. Yet we must ask ourselves whether its full force has not been attenuated by a relativistic approach to Christian doctrine similar to that found in secular ideologies, which, in alleging that science alone is "objective," relegate religion entirely to the subjective sphere of individual feeling. Scientific discoveries, and their application through human ingenuity, undoubtedly offer new possibilities for the betterment of humankind. This does not mean, however, that the "knowable" is limited to the empirically verifiable, nor religion restricted to the shifting realm of "personal experience."

For Christians to accept this faulty line of reasoning would lead to the notion that there is little need to emphasize objective truth in see a symbol of the Church's unity, which is the unity – as Saint Paul has told us – of a living body composed of many different members, each with its own role and purpose. Here too we see our need to acknowledge and reverence the gifts of each and every member of the body as "manifestations of the Spirit given for the good of all" (1 Cor 12:7). Certainly within the Church's divinely-willed structure there is a distinction to be made between hierarchical and charismatic gifts (cf. *Lumen Gentium*, 4). Yet the very variety and richness of the graces bestowed by the Spirit invite us constantly to discern how these gifts are to be rightly ordered in the service of the Church's mission. You, dear priests, by sacramental ordination have been configured to Christ, the Head of the Body. You, dear deacons, have been ordained for the service of that Body. You, dear men and women religious, both contemplative and apostolic, have devoted your lives to following the divine Master in generous love and complete devotion to his Gospel. All of you, who fill this cathedral today, as well as your retired, elderly and infirm brothers and sisters, who unite their prayers and sacrifices to your labors, are called to be forces of unity within Christ's Body. By your personal witness, and your fidelity to the ministry or apostolate entrusted to you, you prepare a path for the Spirit. For the Spirit never ceases to pour out his abundant gifts, to awaken new vocations and missions, and to guide the Church, as our Lord promised in this morning's Gospel, into the fullness of truth (cf. Jn 16:13).

So let us lift our gaze upward! And with great humility and confidence, let us ask the Spirit to enable us each day to grow in the holiness that will make us living stones in the temple which he is even now raising up in the midst of our world. If we are to be true forces of unity, let us be the first to seek inner reconciliation through penance. Let us forgive the wrongs we have suffered and put aside all anger and contention. Let us be the first to demonstrate the humility and purity of heart which are required to approach the splendor of God's truth. In fidelity to the deposit of faith entrusted to the Apostles (cf. 1 Tim 6:20), let us be joyful witnesses of the transforming power of the Gospel!

Dear brothers and sisters, in the finest traditions of the Church in this country, may you also be the first friend of the poor, the homeless, the stranger, the sick and all who suffer. Act as beacons of hope, casting the light of Christ upon the world, and encouraging young people to discover the beauty of a life given completely to the Lord and his Church. I make this plea in a particular way to the many seminarians and young religious present. All of you have a special place in my heart. Never forget that you are called to carry on, with all the enthusiasm and joy that the Spirit has given you, a work that others have begun, a legacy that one day you too will have to pass on to a new generation. Work generously and joyfully, for he whom you serve is the Lord!

The spires of Saint Patrick's Cathedral are dwarfed by the skyscrapers of the Manhattan skyline, yet in the heart of this busy metropolis, they are a vivid reminder of the constant yearning of the human spirit to rise to God. As we celebrate this Eucharist, let us thank the Lord for allowing us to know him in the communion of the Church, to cooperate in building up his Mystical Body, and in bringing his saving word as good news to the men and women of our time. And when we leave this great church, let us go forth as heralds of hope in the midst of this city, and all those places where God's grace

has placed us. In this way, the Church in America will know a new springtime in the Spirit, and point the way to that other, greater city, the new Jerusalem, whose light is the Lamb (Rev 21:23). For there God is even now preparing for all people a banquet of unending joy and life. Amen.

Words spoken spontaneously by the Holy Father at the conclusion of the Holy Mass:

At this moment I can only thank you for your love of the Church and Our Lord, and for the love which you show to the poor Successor of Saint Peter. I will try to do all that is possible to be a worthy successor of the great Apostle, who also was a man with faults and sins, but remained in the end the rock for the Church. And so I too, with all my spiritual poverty, can be for this time, in virtue of the Lord's grace, the Successor of Peter.

It is also your prayers and your love which give me the certainty that the Lord will help me in this my ministry. I am therefore deeply grateful for your love and for your prayers. My response now for all that you have given to me during this visit is my blessing, which I impart to you at the conclusion of this beautiful celebration.

MEETING WITH YOUNG PEOPLE HAVING DISABILITIES

WORDS OF HIS HOLINESS BENEDICT XVI

Saint Joseph Seminary, Yonkers, New York
Saturday, April 19, 2008

Your Eminence,
Bishop Walsh,
Dear Friends,

I am very happy to have this opportunity to spend a brief moment with you. I thank Cardinal Egan for his welcome and especially thank your representatives for their kind words and for the gift of the drawing. Know that it is a special joy for me to be with you. Please give my greetings to your parents and family members, and your teachers and caregivers.

God has blessed you with life, and with differing talents and gifts. Through these you are able to serve him and society in various ways. While some people's contributions seem great and others more modest, the witness value of our efforts is always a sign of hope for everyone.

Sometimes it is challenging to find a reason for what appears only as a difficulty to be overcome or even pain to be endured. Yet our faith helps us to break open the horizon beyond our own selves in order to see life as God does. God's unconditional love, which bathes every human individual, points to a meaning and purpose for all human life. Through his Cross, Jesus in fact draws us into his saving love (cf. Jn 12:32) and in so doing shows us the way ahead - the way of hope which transfigures us all, so that we too, become bearers of that hope and charity for others.

Dear friends, I encourage you all to pray every day for our world. There are so many intentions and people you can pray for, including those who have yet to come to know Jesus. And please do continue to pray for me. As you know I have just had another birthday. Time passes!

Thank you all again, including the Cathedral of Saint Patrick Young Singers and the members of the Archdiocesan Deaf Choir. As a sign of strength and peace and with great affection in our Lord, I impart to you and your families, teachers and caregivers my Apostolic Blessing.

MEETING WITH YOUNG PEOPLE AND SEMINARIANS

ADDRESS OF HIS HOLINESS BENEDICT XVI

Saint Joseph Seminary, Yonkers, New York
Saturday, April 19, 2008

Your Eminence,
Dear Brother Bishops,
Dear Young Friends,

"Proclaim the Lord Christ … and always have your answer ready for people who ask the reason for the hope that is within you" (1 Pet 3:15). With these words from the First Letter of Peter I greet each of you with heartfelt affection. I thank Cardinal Egan for his kind words of welcome and I also thank the representatives chosen from among you for their gestures of welcome. To Bishop Walsh, Rector of Saint Joseph Seminary, staff and seminarians, I offer my special greetings and gratitude.

Young friends, I am very happy to have the opportunity to speak with you. Please pass on my warm greetings to your family members and relatives, and to the teachers and staff of the various schools, colleges and universities you attend. I know that many people have worked hard to ensure that our gathering could take place. I am most grateful to them all. Also, I wish to acknowledge your singing to me Happy Birthday! Thank you for this moving gesture; I give you all an "A plus" for your German pronunciation! This evening I wish to share with you some thoughts about being disciples of Jesus Christ walking in the Lord's footsteps, our own lives become a journey of hope.

In front of you are the images of six ordinary men and women who grew up to lead extraordinary lives. The Church honors them as Venerable, Blessed, or Saint: each responded to the Lord's call to a life of charity and each served him here, in the alleys, streets and suburbs of New York. I am struck by what a remarkably diverse group they are: poor and rich, lay men and women - one a wealthy wife and mother - priests and sisters, immigrants from afar, the daughter of a Mohawk warrior father and Algonquin mother, another a Haitian slave, and a Cuban intellectual.

Saint Elizabeth Ann Seton, Saint Frances Xavier Cabrini, Saint John Neumann, Blessed Kateri Tekakwitha, Venerable Pierre Toussaint, and Padre Felix Varela: any one of us could be among them,

for there is no stereotype to this group, no single mold. Yet a closer look reveals that there are common elements. Inflamed with the love of Jesus, their lives became remarkable journeys of hope. For some, that meant leaving home and embarking on a pilgrim journey of thousands of miles. For each there was an act of abandonment to God, in the confidence that he is the final destination of every pilgrim. And all offered an outstretched hand of hope to those they encountered along the way, often awakening in them a life of faith. Through orphanages, schools and hospitals, by befriending the poor, the sick and the marginalized, and through the compelling witness that comes from walking humbly in the footsteps of Jesus, these six people laid open the way of faith, hope and charity to countless individuals, including perhaps your own ancestors.

And what of today? Who bears witness to the Good News of Jesus on the streets of New York, in the troubled neighborhoods of large cities, in the places where the young gather, seeking someone in whom they can trust? God is our origin and our destination, and Jesus the way. The path of that journey twists and turns   just as it did for our saints   through the joys and the trials of ordinary, everyday life: within your families, at school or college, during your recreation activities, and in your parish communities. All these places are marked by the culture in which you are growing up. As young Americans you are offered many opportunities for personal development, and you are brought up with a sense of generosity, service and fairness. Yet you do not need me to tell you that there are also difficulties: activities and mindsets which stifle hope, pathways which seem to lead to happiness and fulfillment but in fact end only in confusion and fear.

My own years as a teenager were marred by a sinister regime that thought it had all the answers; its influence grew – infiltrating schools and civic bodies, as well as politics and even religion – before it was fully recognized for the monster it was. It banished God and thus became impervious to anything true and good. Many of your grandparents and great-grandparents will have recounted the horror of the destruction that ensued. Indeed, some of them came to America precisely to escape such terror.

Let us thank God that today many people of your generation are able to enjoy the liberties which have arisen through the extension of democracy and respect for human rights. Let us thank God for all those who strive to ensure that you can grow up in an environment that nurtures what is beautiful, good, and true: your parents and grandparents, your teachers and priests, those civic leaders who seek what is right and just.

The power to destroy does, however, remain. To pretend otherwise would be to fool ourselves. Yet, it never triumphs; it is defeated. This is the essence of the hope that defines us as Christians; and the Church recalls this most dramatically during the Easter Triduum and celebrates it with great joy in the season of Easter! The One who shows us the way beyond death is the One who shows us how to overcome destruction and fear: thus it is Jesus who is the true teacher of life (cf. *Spe Salvi*, 6). His death and resurrection mean that we can say to the Father "you have restored us to life!" (Prayer after Communion, Good Friday). And so, just a few weeks ago, during the beautiful Easter Vigil liturgy, it was not from despair or fear that we cried out to God for our world, but with hope-filled confidence: dispel the darkness of our heart! dispel the darkness of our minds! (cf. Prayer at the Lighting of the Easter Candle).

What might that darkness be? What happens when people, especially the most vulnerable, encounter a clenched fist of repression or manipulation rather than a hand of hope? A first group of examples pertains to the heart. Here, the dreams and longings that young people pursue can so easily be shattered or destroyed. I am thinking of those affected by drug and substance abuse, homelessness and poverty, racism, violence, and degradation – especially of girls and women. While the causes of these problems are complex, all have in common a poisoned attitude of mind which results in people being treated as mere objects; a callousness of heart takes hold which first ignores, then ridicules, the God-given dignity of every human being. Such tragedies also point to what might have been and what could be, were there other hands – your hands – reaching out. I encourage you to invite others, especially the vulnerable and the innocent, to join you along the way of goodness and hope.

The second area of darkness – that which affects the mind – often goes unnoticed, and for this reason is particularly sinister. The manipulation of truth distorts our perception of reality, and tarnishes our imagination and aspirations. I have already mentioned the many liberties which you are fortunate enough to enjoy. The fundamental importance of freedom must be rigorously safeguarded. It is no surprise then that numerous individuals and groups vociferously claim their freedom in the public forum. Yet freedom is a delicate value. It can be misunderstood or misused so as to lead not to the happiness which we all expect it to yield, but to a dark arena of manipulation in which our understanding of self and the world becomes confused, or even distorted by those who have an ulterior agenda.

Have you noticed how often the call for freedom is made without ever referring to the truth of the human person? Some today argue that respect for freedom of the individual makes it wrong to seek truth, including the truth about what is good. In some circles to speak of truth is seen as controversial or divisive, and consequently best kept in the private sphere. And in truth's place – or better said its absence – an idea has spread which, in giving value to everything indiscriminately, claims to assure freedom and to liberate conscience. This we call relativism. But what purpose has a "freedom" which, in disregarding truth, pursues what is false or wrong? How many young people have been offered a hand which in the name of freedom or experience has led them to addiction, to moral or intellectual confusion, to hurt, to a loss of self-respect, even to despair and so tragically and sadly to the taking of their own life? Dear friends, truth is not an imposition. Nor is it simply a set of rules. It is a discovery of the One who never fails us; the One whom we can always trust. In seeking truth we come to live by belief because ultimately truth is a person: Jesus Christ. That is why authentic freedom is not an opting out. It is an opting in; nothing less than letting go of self and allowing oneself to be drawn into Christ's very being for others (cf. Spe Salvi, 28).

How then can we as believers help others to walk the path of freedom which brings fulfillment and lasting happiness? Let us again turn to the saints. How did their witness truly free others from the darkness of heart and mind? The answer is found in the kernel of their faith; the kernel of our faith. The Incarnation, the birth of Jesus, tells us that God

does indeed find a place among us. Though the inn is full, he enters through the stable, and there are people who see his light. They recognize Herod's dark closed world for what it is, and instead follow the bright guiding star of the night sky. And what shines forth? Here you might recall the prayer uttered on the most holy night of Easter: "Father, we share in the light of your glory through your Son the light of the world … inflame us with your hope!" (Blessing of the Fire). And so, in solemn procession with our lighted candles we pass the light of Christ among us. It is "the light which dispels all evil, washes guilt away, restores lost innocence, brings mourners joy, casts out hatred, brings us peace, and humbles earthly pride" (Exsultet). This is Christ's light at work. This is the way of the saints. It is a magnificent vision of hope – Christ's light beckons you to be guiding stars for others, walking Christ's way of forgiveness, reconciliation, humility, joy and peace.

At times, however, we are tempted to close in on ourselves, to doubt the strength of Christ's radiance, to limit the horizon of hope. Take courage! Fix your gaze on our saints. The diversity of their experience of God's presence prompts us to discover anew the breadth and depth of Christianity. Let your imaginations soar freely along the limitless expanse of the horizons of Christian discipleship. Sometimes we are looked upon as people who speak only of prohibitions. Nothing could be further from the truth! Authentic Christian discipleship is marked by a sense of wonder. We stand before the God we know and love as a friend, the vastness of his creation, and the beauty of our Christian faith.

Dear friends, the example of the saints invites us, then, to consider four essential aspects of the treasure of our faith: personal prayer and silence, liturgical prayer, charity in action, and vocations.

What matters most is that you develop your personal relationship with God. That relationship is expressed in prayer. God by his very nature speaks, hears, and replies. Indeed, Saint Paul reminds us: we can and should "pray constantly" (1 Thess 5:17). Far from turning in on ourselves or withdrawing from the ups and downs of life, by praying we turn towards God and through him to each other, including the marginalized and those following ways other than God's path (cf. Spe Salvi, 33). As the saints teach us so vividly, prayer becomes hope in action. Christ was their constant companion, with whom they conversed at every step of their journey for others.

There is another aspect of prayer which we need to remember: silent contemplation. Saint John, for example, tells us that to embrace God's revelation we must first listen, then respond by proclaiming what we have heard and seen (cf. 1 Jn 1:2-3; Dei Verbum, 1). Have we perhaps lost something of the art of listening? Do you leave space to hear God's whisper, calling you forth into goodness? Friends, do not be afraid of silence or stillness, listen to God, adore him in the Eucharist. Let his word shape your journey as an unfolding of holiness.

In the liturgy we find the whole Church at prayer. The word liturgy means the participation of God's people in "the work of Christ the Priest and of His Body which is the Church" (Sacrosanctum Concilium, 7). What is that work? First of all it refers to Christ's Passion, his Death and Resurrection, and his Ascension – what we call the Paschal Mystery. It also refers to the celebration of the liturgy itself. The two meanings are in fact inseparably linked because this "work of

Jesus" is the real content of the liturgy. Through the liturgy, the "work of Jesus" is continually brought into contact with history; with our lives in order to shape them. Here we catch another glimpse of the grandeur of our Christian faith. Whenever you gather for Mass, when you go to Confession, whenever you celebrate any of the sacraments, Jesus is at work. Through the Holy Spirit, he draws you to himself, into his sacrificial love of the Father which becomes love for all. We see then that the Church's liturgy is a ministry of hope for humanity. Your faithful participation, is an active hope which helps to keep the world – saints and sinners alike – open to God; this is the truly human hope we offer everyone (cf. *Spe Salvi*, 34).

Your personal prayer, your times of silent contemplation, and your participation in the Church's liturgy, bring you closer to God and also prepare you to serve others. The saints accompanying us this evening show us that the life of faith and hope is also a life of charity. Contemplating Jesus on the Cross we see love in its most radical form. We can begin to imagine the path of love along which we must move (cf. *Deus Caritas Est*, 12). The opportunities to make this journey are abundant. Look about you with Christ's eyes, listen with his ears, feel and think with his heart and mind. Are you ready to give all as he did for truth and justice? Many of the examples of the suffering which our saints responded to with compassion are still found here in this city and beyond. And new injustices have arisen: some are complex and stem from the exploitation of the heart and manipulation of the mind; even our common habitat, the earth itself, groans under the weight of consumerist greed and irresponsible exploitation. We must listen deeply. We must respond with a renewed social action that stems from the universal love that knows no bounds. In this way, we ensure that our works of mercy and justice become hope in action for others.

Dear young people, finally I wish to share a word about vocations. First of all my thoughts go to your parents, grandparents and godparents. They have been your primary educators in the faith. By presenting you for baptism, they made it possible for you to receive the greatest gift of your life. On that day you entered into the holiness of God himself. You became adoptive sons and daughters of the Father. You were incorporated into Christ. You were made a dwelling place of his Spirit. Let us pray for mothers and fathers throughout the world, particularly those who may be struggling in any way – socially, materially, spiritually. Let us honor the vocation of matrimony and the dignity of family life. Let us always appreciate that it is in families that vocations are given life.

Gathered here at Saint Joseph Seminary, I greet the seminarians present and indeed encourage all seminarians throughout America. I am glad to know that your numbers are increasing! The People of God look to you to be holy priests, on a daily journey of conversion, inspiring in others the desire to enter more deeply into the ecclesial life of believers. I urge you to deepen your friendship with Jesus the Good Shepherd. Talk heart to heart with him. Reject any temptation to ostentation, careerism, or conceit. Strive for a pattern of life truly marked by charity, chastity and humility, in imitation of Christ, the Eternal High Priest, of whom you are to become living icons (cf. *Pastores Dabo Vobis*, 33). Dear seminarians, I pray for you daily. Remember that what counts before the Lord is to dwell in his love and to make his love shine forth for others.

Religious sisters, brothers and priests contribute greatly to the mission of the Church. Their prophetic witness is marked by a profound conviction of the primacy with which the Gospel shapes Christian life and transforms society. Today, I wish to draw your attention to the positive spiritual renewal which congregations are undertaking in relation to their charism. The word *charism* means a gift freely and graciously given. Charisms are bestowed by the Holy Spirit, who inspires founders and foundresses, and shapes congregations with a subsequent spiritual heritage. The wondrous array of charisms proper to each religious institute is an extraordinary spiritual treasury. Indeed, the history of the Church is perhaps most beautifully portrayed through the history of her schools of spirituality, most of which stem from the saintly lives of founders and foundresses. Through the discovery of charisms, which yield such a breadth of spiritual wisdom, I am sure that some of you young people will be drawn to a life of apostolic or contemplative service. Do not be shy to speak with religious brothers, sisters or priests about the charism and spirituality of their congregation. No perfect community exists, but it is fidelity to a founding charism, not to particular individuals, that the Lord calls you to discern. Have courage! You too can make your life a gift of self for the love of the Lord Jesus and, in him, of every member of the human family (cf. Vita Consecrata, 3).

Friends, again I ask you, what about today? What are you seeking? What is God whispering to you? The hope which never disappoints is Jesus Christ. The saints show us the selfless love of his way. As disciples of Christ, their extraordinary journeys unfolded within the community of hope, which is the Church. It is from within the Church that you too will find the courage and support to walk the way of the Lord. Nourished by personal prayer, prompted in silence, shaped by the Church's liturgy, you will discover the particular vocation God has for you. Embrace it with joy. You are Christ's disciples today. Shine his light upon this great city and beyond. Show the world the reason for the hope that resonates within you. Tell others about the truth that sets you free. With these sentiments of great hope in you I bid you farewell, until we meet again in Sydney this July for World Youth Day! And as a pledge of my love for you and your families, I gladly impart my Apostolic Blessing.

VISIT TO GROUND ZERO

PRAYER OF HIS HOLINESS BENEDICT XVI

Ground Zero, New York
Sunday, April 20, 2008

O God of love, compassion, and healing,
look on us, people of many different faiths and traditions,
who gather today at this site,
the scene of incredible violence and pain.

We ask you in your goodness
to give eternal light and peace
to all who died here—
the heroic first-responders:
our fire fighters, police officers,
emergency service workers, and Port Authority personnel,
along with all the innocent men and women
who were victims of this tragedy
simply because their work or service
brought them here on September 11, 2001.

We ask you, in your compassion
to bring healing to those
who, because of their presence here that day,
suffer from injuries and illness.
Heal, too, the pain of still-grieving families
and all who lost loved ones in this tragedy.
Give them strength to continue their lives with courage and hope.

We are mindful as well
of those who suffered death, injury, and loss
on the same day at the Pentagon and in Shanksville, Pennsylvania.
Our hearts are one with theirs
as our prayer embraces their pain and suffering.

God of peace, bring your peace to our violent world:
peace in the hearts of all men and women
and peace among the nations of the earth.
Turn to your way of love
those whose hearts and minds
are consumed with hatred.

God of understanding,
overwhelmed by the magnitude of this tragedy,
we seek your light and guidance
as we confront such terrible events.
Grant that those whose lives were spared
may live so that the lives lost here
may not have been lost in vain.
Comfort and console us,
strengthen us in hope,
and give us the wisdom and courage
to work tirelessly for a world
where true peace and love reign
among nations and in the hearts of all.

CELEBRATION OF THE EUCHARIST

HOMILY OF HIS HOLINESS BENEDICT XVI

Yankee Stadium, Bronx, New York
Fifth Sunday of Easter, April 20, 2008

Dear Brothers and Sisters in Christ,

In the Gospel we have just heard, Jesus tells his Apostles to put their faith in him, for he is "the way, and the truth and the life" (Jn 14:6). Christ is the way that leads to the Father, the truth which gives meaning to human existence, and the source of that life which is eternal joy with all the saints in his heavenly Kingdom. Let us take the Lord at his word! Let us renew our faith in him and put all our hope in his promises!

With this encouragement to persevere in the faith of Peter (cf. Lk 22:32; Mt 16:17), I greet all of you with great affection. I thank Cardinal Egan for his cordial words of welcome in your name. At this Mass, the Church in the United States celebrates the two hundredth anniversary of the creation of the Sees of New York, Boston, Philadelphia and Louisville from the mother See of Baltimore. The presence around this altar of the Successor of Peter, his brother bishops and priests, and deacons, men and women religious, and lay faithful from throughout the fifty states of the Union, eloquently manifests our communion in the Catholic faith which comes to us from the Apostles.

Our celebration today is also a sign of the impressive growth which God has given to the Church in your country in the past two hundred years. From a small flock like that described in the first reading, the Church in America has been built up in fidelity to the twin commandment of love of God and love of neighbor. In this land of freedom and opportunity, the Church has united a widely diverse flock in the profession of the faith and, through her many educational, charitable and social works, has also contributed significantly to the growth of American society as a whole.

This great accomplishment was not without its challenges. Today's first reading, taken from the Acts of the Apostles, speaks of linguistic and cultural tensions already present within the earliest Church community. At the same time, it shows the power of the word of God, authoritatively proclaimed by the Apostles and received in faith, to create a unity which transcends the divisions arising from human limitations and weakness. Here we are reminded of a fundamental truth: that the Church's unity has no other basis than the Word of God, made flesh in Christ Jesus our Lord. All external signs of identity, all structures, associations and programs, valuable or even essential as they may be, ultimately exist only to support and foster the deeper unity which, in Christ, is God's indefectible gift to his Church.

The first reading also makes clear, as we see from the imposition of hands on the first deacons, that the Church's unity is "apostolic." It is a visible unity, grounded in the Apostles whom Christ chose and appointed as witnesses to his resurrection, and it is born of what the Scriptures call "the obedience of faith" (Rom 1:5; cf. Acts 6:7).

"Authority" ... "obedience." To be frank, these are not easy words speak nowadays. Words like these represent a "stumbling stone" many of our contemporaries, especially in a society which rightly aces a high value on personal freedom. Yet, in the light of our faith Jesus Christ – "the way and the truth and the life" – we come to see fullest meaning, value, and indeed beauty, of those words. The ospel teaches us that true freedom, the freedom of the children of od, is found only in the self-surrender which is part of the mystery love. Only by losing ourselves, the Lord tells us, do we truly find rselves (cf. Lk 17:33). True freedom blossoms when we turn away m the burden of sin, which clouds our perceptions and weakens r resolve, and find the source of our ultimate happiness in him who nfinite love, infinite freedom, infinite life. "In his will is our peace."

Real freedom, then, is God's gracious gift, the fruit of conversion his truth, the truth which makes us free (cf. Jn 8:32). And this free-m in truth brings in its wake a new and liberating way of seeing ality. When we put on "the mind of Christ" (cf. Phil 2:5), new hori-ns open before us! In the light of faith, within the communion of the urch, we also find the inspiration and strength to become a leaven the Gospel in the world. We become the light of the world, the t of the earth (cf. Mt 5:13-14), entrusted with the "apostolate" of aking our own lives, and the world in which we live, conform ever re fully to God's saving plan.

This magnificent vision of a world being transformed by the liber-ng truth of the Gospel is reflected in the description of the Church und in today's second reading. The Apostle tells us that Christ, risen m the dead, is the keystone of a great temple which is even now ng in the Spirit. And we, the members of his Body, through bap-m have become "living stones" in that temple, sharing in the life of od by grace, blessed with the freedom of the sons of God, and npowered to offer spiritual sacrifices pleasing to him (cf. 1 Pet 2:5). d what is this offering which we are called to make, if not to direct r every thought, word and action to the truth of the Gospel and to rness all our energies in the service of God's Kingdom? Only in this ay can we build with God, on the one foundation which is Christ . 1 Cor 3:11). Only in this way can we build something that will ly endure. Only in this way can our lives find ultimate meaning and ur lasting fruit.

Today we recall the bicentennial of a watershed in the history of e Church in the United States: its first great chapter of growth. In ese two hundred years, the face of the Catholic community in your untry has changed greatly. We think of the successive waves of migrants whose traditions have so enriched the Church in America. e think of the strong faith which built up the network of churches, ucational, healthcare and social institutions which have long been e hallmark of the Church in this land. We think also of those count-s fathers and mothers who passed on the faith to their children, the eady ministry of the many priests who devoted their lives to the care souls, and the incalculable contribution made by so many men and omen religious, who not only taught generations of children how to ad and write, but also inspired in them a lifelong desire to know od, to love him and to serve him. How many "spiritual sacrifices easing to God" have been offered up in these two centuries! In this d of religious liberty, Catholics found freedom not only to practice eir faith, but also to participate fully in civic life, bringing their deep-

est moral convictions to the public square and cooperating with their neighbors in shaping a vibrant, democratic society. Today's celebra-tion is more than an occasion of gratitude for graces received. It is also a summons to move forward with firm resolve to use wisely the blessings of freedom, in order to build a future of hope for coming generations.

"You are a chosen race, a royal priesthood, a holy nation, a people he claims for his own, to proclaim his glorious works" (1 Pet 2:9). These words of the Apostle Peter do not simply remind us of the dignity which is ours by God's grace; they also challenge us to an ever greater fidelity to the glorious inheritance which we have received in Christ (cf. Eph 1:18). They challenge us to examine our consciences, to purify our hearts, to renew our baptismal commitment to reject Satan and all his empty promises. They challenge us to be a people of joy, heralds of the unfailing hope (cf. Rom 5:5) born of faith in God's word, and trust in his promises.

Each day, throughout this land, you and so many of your neigh-bors pray to the Father in the Lord's own words: "Thy Kingdom come." This prayer needs to shape the mind and heart of every Christian in this nation. It needs to bear fruit in the way you lead your lives and in the way you build up your families and your communities. It needs to create new "settings of hope" (cf. *Spe Salvi*, 32ff.) where God's Kingdom becomes present in all its saving power.

Praying fervently for the coming of the Kingdom also means being constantly alert for the signs of its presence, and working for its growth in every sector of society. It means facing the challenges of present and future with confidence in Christ's victory and a commitment to extending his reign. It means not losing heart in the face of resis-tance, adversity and scandal. It means overcoming every separation between faith and life, and countering false gospels of freedom and happiness. It also means rejecting a false dichotomy between faith and political life, since, as the Second Vatican Council put it, "there is no human activity – even in secular affairs – which can be withdrawn from God's dominion" (*Lumen Gentium*, 36). It means working to enrich American society and culture with the beauty and truth of the Gospel, and never losing sight of that great hope which gives mean-ing and value to all the other hopes which inspire our lives.

And this, dear friends, is the particular challenge which the Suc-cessor of Saint Peter sets before you today. As "a chosen people, a royal priesthood, a holy nation," follow faithfully in the footsteps of those who have gone before you! Hasten the coming of God's Kingdom in this land! Past generations have left you an impressive legacy. In our day too, the Catholic community in this nation has been outstanding in its prophetic witness in the defense of life, in the education of the young, in care for the poor, the sick and the stranger in your midst. On these solid foundations, the future of the Church in America must even now begin to rise!

Yesterday, not far from here, I was moved by the joy, the hope and the generous love of Christ which I saw on the faces of the many young people assembled in Dunwoodie. They are the Church's future, and they deserve all the prayer and support that you can give them. And so I wish to close by adding a special word of encouragement to them. My dear young friends, like the seven men, "filled with the Spirit and wisdom" whom the Apostles charged with care for the young Church, may you step forward and take up the responsibility which your faith in Christ sets before you! May you find the courage to proclaim Christ, "the same, yesterday, and today and for ever" and the unchanging truths which have their foundation in him (cf. *Gaudium et Spes*, 10; Heb 13:8). These are the truths that set us free! They are the truths which alone can guarantee respect for the inalienable dignity and rights of each man, woman and child in our world – including the most defenseless of all human beings, the unborn child in the mother's womb. In a world where, as Pope John Paul II, speaking in this very place, reminded us, Lazarus continues to stand at our door (Homily at Yankee Stadium, October 2, 1979, No. 7), let your faith and love bear rich fruit in outreach to the poor, the needy and those without a voice. Young men and women of America, I urge you: open your hearts to the Lord's call to follow him in the priesthood and the religious life. Can there be any greater mark of love than this: to follow in the footsteps of Christ, who was willing to lay down his life for his friends (cf. Jn 15:13)?

In today's Gospel, the Lord promises his disciples that they will perform works even greater than his (cf. Jn 14:12). Dear friends, only God in his providence knows what works his grace has yet to bring forth in your lives and in the life of the Church in the United States. Yet Christ's promise fills us with sure hope. Let us now join our prayers to his, as living stones in that spiritual temple which is his one, holy, catholic and apostolic Church. Let us lift our eyes to him, for even now he is preparing for us a place in his Father's house. And empowered by his Holy Spirit, let us work with renewed zeal for the spread of his Kingdom.

"Happy are you who believe!" (cf. 1 Pet 2:7). Let us turn to Jesus! He alone is the way that leads to eternal happiness, the truth who satisfies the deepest longings of every heart, and the life who brings ever new joy and hope, to us and to our world. Amen.

FAREWELL CEREMONY

ADDRESS OF HIS HOLINESS BENEDICT XVI

John Fitzgerald Kennedy International Airport, New York
Sunday, April 20, 2008

Mr. Vice-President,
Distinguished Civil Authorities,
My Brother Bishops,
Dear Brothers and Sisters,

The time has come for me to bid farewell to your country. These days that I have spent in the United States have been blessed with many memorable experiences of American hospitality, and I wish to express my deep appreciation to all of you for your kind welcome. It has been a joy for me to witness the faith and devotion of the Catholic community here. It was heart-warming to spend time with leaders and representatives of other Christian communities and other religions, and I renew my assurances of respect and esteem to all of you. I am grateful to President Bush for kindly coming to greet me at the start of

my visit, and I thank Vice-President Cheney for his presence here [ ] I depart. The civic authorities, workers and volunteers in Washing[ ] and New York have given generously of their time and resources order to ensure the smooth progress of my visit at every stage, and this I express my profound thanks and appreciation to Mayor Adri Fenty of Washington and Mayor Michael Bloomberg of New Yor[ ]

Once again I offer prayerful good wishes to the representativ of the see of Baltimore, the first Archdiocese, and those of Ne York, Boston, Philadelphia and Louisville, in this jubilee year. M the Lord continue to bless you in the years ahead. To all my Brot[ ] Bishops, to Bishop DiMarzio of this Diocese of Brooklyn, and to [ ] officers and staff of the Episcopal Conference who have contribut in so many ways to the preparation of this visit, I extend my renew gratitude for their hard work and dedication. With great affectio greet once more the priests and religious, the deacons, the semin ians and young people, and all the faithful in the United States, an encourage you to continue bearing joyful witness to Christ our Hop our Risen Lord and Savior, who makes all things new and gives life in abundance.

One of the high-points of my visit was the opportunity to addre the General Assembly of the United Nations, and I thank Secreta General Ban Ki-moon for his kind invitation and welcome. Looki back over the sixty years that have passed since the Universal Dec ration of Human Rights, I give thanks for all that the Organization h been able to achieve in defending and promoting the fundamen rights of every man, woman and child throughout the world, anc encourage people of good will everywhere to continue working ti lessly to promote justice and peaceful co-existence between peop and nations.

My visit this morning to Ground Zero will remain firmly etched my memory, as I continue to pray for those who died and for all w suffer in consequence of the tragedy that occurred there in 2001. F all the people of America, and indeed throughout the world, I pr that the future will bring increased fraternity and solidarity, a grow in mutual respect, and a renewed trust and confidence in God, c heavenly Father.

With these words, I take my leave, I ask you to remember me your prayers, and I assure you of my affection and friendship in t Lord. May God bless America!